D0699833

Careers in Focus

Physicians

Ferguson Publishing Company
Chicago, Illinois

Copyright © 2000 Ferguson Publishing Company
ISBN 0-89434-315-7

Printed in the United States of America

Cover photo courtesy Tony Stone Images

Published and distributed by
Ferguson Publishing Company
200 West Jackson Street, 7th Floor
Chicago, Illinois 60606
800-306-9941
www.fergpubco.com

All rights reserved. No part of this publication may be reproduced, stored in
a retrieval system, or transmitted by any means, electronic, mechanical, pho-
tocopying or otherwise, without the prior permission of the publisher.

Y - 6

Table of Contents

Introduction

The single most familiar element of the medical industry is the physician. For many years, the main health consultant was the family physician. General practitioners still serve the role of the family doctor to many families in the United States, but the role and the method of medical care delivery by the family doctor has changed.

According to the U.S. Department of Labor, less than 12 percent of the physicians in the United States are general or family practitioners. General practitioners will handle most medical problems, but when an emergency or problem arises that the family doctor may not have the equipment or capability to handle, the patient is referred to a specialist. The patient may rely on his or her generalist to recommend a specialist, or the patient may be able in some cases to determine which type of specialist is needed. For skin problems, for example, most patients would go to a dermatologist.

Internists, who account for about 16 percent of all physicians in the United States, are frequently used as general practitioners. They are capable of handling most medical concerns that are presented to them by their patients and will make referrals to specialists as needed. There are at least 40 different specialties for the physician to choose from while in medical school. They range from anesthesiology to urology. About one-quarter of the practicing physicians specialize in some aspect of surgery. The rest work in one specific area of the body, one specific element of treatment, or with one specific clientele. For example, pediatricians work with children; neurologists work with problems of the nervous system; and anesthesiologists handle anesthetization during surgical procedures. About 6 percent of physicians are psychiatrists.

Earnings for physicians are among the highest of any occupation. Physicians also spend the longest time preparing for their careers and their education, therefore, is expensive. All physicians must earn a bachelor's degree and then apply to medical school. Four years of medical school leads to an M.D. (doctor of medicine) degree or D.O. (doctor of osteopathy), after which students must pass an exam that certifies them to practice medicine. Then they complete a one- to two-year internship. The internship is followed by a residency, which takes from one to seven years depending on the specialty. Subspecialties (i.e., vascular surgery is a subspecialty of surgery and reproductive endocrinology is a subspecialty of obstetrics/gynecology) require additional training, usually called a fellowship, that can take one to three years. The training is long and intense, but the rewards are great, both in terms of job satisfaction and financial compensation.

Physicians earn an average salary of $160,000. At the lower end of the scale, general practitioners earn $132,000. Cardiologists earn $186,000, geriatricians earn $200,000, obstetricians/gynecologists earn $231,000, psychiatrists earn $138,000, and surgeons earn $275,000. Dentists' salaries average around $120,000 and dental specialists earn around $175,000.

According to U.S. government projections, the health care industry will be the fastest growing sector of the economy, creating 4.2 million new jobs by 2006.

The employment outlook for physicians is expected to be better than average from 1990 to 2005. The number of physicians will grow by about 34 percent, from about 580,000 in 1990 to 776,000 by 2006. More doctors will be needed because the population is both growing and aging. Also, many new technological improvements may require the expertise of greater numbers of medical specialists. However, the need for primary care providers will be far greater than the need for medical specialists. Job prospects will be best in internal medicine, family practice, geriatrics, and preventive medicine.

Each article in this book discusses a particular physician occupation in detail. The information comes from Ferguson's *Encyclopedia of Careers and Vocational Guidance.* The History section describes the history of the particular job as it relates to the overall development of its industry or field. The Job describes the primary and secondary duties of the job. Requirements discusses high school and postsecondary education and training requirements, any certification or licensing necessary, and any other personal requirements for success in the job. Exploring* offers suggestions on how to gain some experience in or knowledge of the particular job before making a firm educational and financial commitment. The focus is on what can be done while still in high school (or in the early years of college) to gain a better understanding of the job. The Employers* section gives an overview of typical places of employment for the job. Starting Out* discusses the best ways to land that first job, be it through the college placement office, newspaper ads, or personal contact. The Advancement* section describes what kind of career path to expect from the job and how to get there. Earnings lists salary ranges and describes the typical fringe benefits. The Work Environment* section describes the typical surroundings and conditions of employment—whether indoors or outdoors, noisy or quiet, social or independent, and so on. Also discussed are typical hours worked, any seasonal fluctuations, and the stresses and strains of the job. The Outlook section summarizes the job in terms of the general economy and industry projections. For the most part, Outlook information is obtained from the Bureau of Labor Statistics and is supplemented by information taken from professional associations. Job growth terms follow those used in the *Occupational Outlook Handbook:* Growth described as "much faster than the average" means an increase of 36 percent or more. Growth described as "faster than the average" means an increase of 21 to 35 percent. Growth described as "about as fast as the average" means an increase of 10 to 20 percent. Growth described as "little change or more slowly than the average" means an increase of 0 to 9 percent. "Decline" means a decrease of 1 percent or more.

Each article ends with For More Information, which lists organizations that can provide career information on training, education, internships, scholarships, and job placement.

* You will see that some of the sections described are missing from the physician specialty articles. That is because the information in those sections is the same as in the Physicians article. If you are interested in a physician specialty, it is suggested that you read the Physicians article first, since all specialists must first become physicians.

Allergists/ Immunologists

Overview

Allergists/immunologists are physicians that specialize in the treatment of allergic, asthmatic, and immunologic diseases. They treat patients with asthma, hay fever, food allergies, AIDS, rheumatoid arthritis, and other diseases.

The Job

Over 20 percent of Americans suffer from some kind of allergy. Allergies to certain foods, plants, pollen, animal fur, air pollution, insects, colognes, chemicals, and cleansers may send sufferers to allergy and immunology specialists, doctors who specialize in the treatment of allergic, asthmatic, and immunologic diseases.

Allergists and immunologists also treat patients with hay fever, also called allergic rhinitis, which causes symptoms such as congestion, sneezing, and a scratchy throat caused by pollens or molds in the air. They treat asthma, a respiratory disease often triggered by an allergic reaction that causes restricted breathing, constricting the air flow to the lungs. Another serious allergic reaction is anaphylaxis. Triggered by a particular food or insect sting, anaphylaxis can quickly restrict breathing, swell the throat, and cause unconsciousness. Other allergies treated by an allergist include skin allergies, such as hives and eczema, and food and drug allergies.

Immunologic diseases are those that affect the immune system. Allergy and immunology specialists treat patients with conditions such as AIDS, rheumatoid arthritis, and lupus. An immunologist will also treat patients who are receiving an organ or bone marrow transplant—to help prevent the patient's body from rejecting the transplanted organ.

Allergists/immunologists listen carefully to the patient and then develop a treatment plan. The doctor reviews the patient's medical history and background, and may also conduct skin tests and blood tests. Skin tests are often preferred because they are inexpensive and the results are available immediately. Skin tests are also better for identifying more subtle allergies.

Once the diagnosis is made, the doctor will determine a treatment plan. In some cases, the solution may be as simple as avoiding the things that cause the allergic reaction. The allergist will help find ways to limit patients' exposure to the allergen. In other cases, a doctor will prescribe medication. Antihistamines are drugs that relieve allergy symptoms such as nasal congestion, eye burning, and skin rashes.

Antihistamines can have side effects such as dizziness, headaches, and nausea. Should these side effects occur, the allergist will treat them and prescribe a new medication. Sometimes a patient can build up a resistance to an antihistamine and the doctor needs to prescribe a stronger variety.

Immunotherapy (a series of allergy shots) is another kind of treatment for asthma and for allergies to pollen, dust, bee venom, and a variety of other substances. Immunotherapy involves injecting the patient with a small amount of the substance that causes the allergic reaction. The immune system then becomes less sensitive to the substances, and reduces the symptoms of allergy. An allergist will give weekly shots over an extended time, gradually increasing the dosage; eventually the shots are only necessary once a month.

Requirements

Postsecondary Training

After earning the M.D. degree and becoming licensed to practice medicine (See *Physicians*), allergists/immunologists must complete a three-year residency in internal medicine or pediatrics, then a minimum of two years of training in an allergy and immunology fellowship. The American Academy of Allergy, Asthma, and Immunology (AAAAI) publishes a training program directory, which lists accredited training programs and faculty and program information.

Certification or Licensing

Certification from the American Board of Allergy and Immunology (ABAI) requires a valid medical license, proof of residency completion, and written evaluation from the residency director. The evaluation reviews the candidate's clinical judgment, attitude, professional behavior, and other work skills and habits. The certification exam tests the candidate's knowledge of the immune system, human pathology, and the molecular basis of allergic and other immune reactions. The candidate must also show an understanding of diagnostic tests and therapy for immunologic diseases.

Other Requirements

Allergists/immunologists should be compassionate, and concerned for the well-being of their patients. They should also be careful listeners—a doctor must have a good understanding of a patient's background, environment, and emotional state to plan the best treatment. An allergist/immunologist must be prepared to deal with the stress of caring for sick patients; some of these patients may have life-threatening diseases such as AIDS, cancer, or severe asthma. Despite the many advances in the treatment of allergic diseases and diseases of the immune system, many of them remain incurable. An allergist/immunologist who deals with severe cases must not become too emotionally involved; a doctor too upset by a patient's illness may not be able to provide the best treatment.

Earnings

Physicians are rewarded well for their years of intensive study, for their long hours, and for their level of responsibility. Allergists/immunologists make from about $50,000 to $200,000 a year. Allergists/immunologists who are still in their residencies may make as little as $25,000 a year. The average annual income for all physicians is $140,000.

Though an allergist/immunologist can make a good living, a number of factors, such as geographical location, experience, and reputation of good work, can determine salary.

Outlook

Employment of physicians will grow faster than average through the year 2006. Over 50 million Americans suffer from some kind of allergy, fueling the demand for allergists/immunologists. This specialty was included in *U.S. News & World Report's* 1998 annual feature, "Best Jobs for the Future." Though some doctors remain skeptical about the relationship between allergy and illness, allergy/immunology has become a respected field of medicine. As this field continues to grow, more doctors will refer their patients to these specialists.

For More Information

For career information and a list of accredited training programs, contact:

American Academy of Allergy, Asthma, and Immunology
611 East Wells Street
Milwaukee, WI 53202
Tel: 414-272-6071
Web: http://www.aaaai.org

American Association of Certified Allergists
85 West Algonquin Road, Suite 550
Arlington Heights, IL 60005
Tel: 847-427-8111

Anesthesiologists

	School Subjects
Biology	
Health	
	Personal Skills
Helping/teaching	
Technical/scientific	
	Work Environment
Primarily indoors	
Primarily multiple locations	
	Minimum Education Level
Medical degree	
	Salary Range
$44,400 to $160,000 to $250,000	
	Certification or Licensing
Required by all states	
	Outlook
Faster than the average	

Overview

Anesthesiologists are physicians who specialize in the planning, performance, and maintenance of a patient's anesthesia during surgical, obstetric, or other medical procedures. Using special equipment, monitors, and drugs, the anesthesiologist makes sure the patient feels no pain and remains uninjured during the procedure.

History

Before the mid-19th century, when modern anesthetics started to be developed, you would most likely live with your affliction or undergo surgery with little or no help for pain. Oftentimes patients would need to be restrained. An 18th century French encyclopedia described how to perform bladder surgery by first restraining the patient in a special "surgical chair."

Efforts to manage pain have been a constant in human history. A variety of substances and techniques have been used, including opium, cannabis, alcohol, mandragora root, and hypnotism. None of these proved entirely reliable or completely effective.

Nitrous oxide, developed in the late 18th century, was the first gas recognized to have anesthetic properties. Its effects, which included giddiness, earned it the nickname of "laughing gas." Ether was developed shortly after nitrous oxide. Neither gas, however, was used to anesthetize humans. In fact, nitrous oxide was often used for entertainment purposes at "laughing gas parties" or by sideshow entertainers.

The first successful use of ether as an anesthetic occurred in 1842 when Dr. Crawford W. Long used it when he removed a tumor from a friend's neck. Dr. Long, however, failed to publicize the event and in 1846 a Boston dentist, Dr. William T. G. Morton, became credited with the discovery of general anesthesia when he successfully administered ether to anesthetize a patient while removing a tumor. As one would imagine, ether's reputation spread quickly. So did the reputation of chloroform, used successfully for the first time in 1847.

Anesthesiology continued to advance and in 1875 intravenous administration of anesthetics was developed. Greater study of anesthesiology in the 20th century has led to many advances and anesthesiology has become increasingly more sophisticated—revolutionizing the practice of surgery.

The Job

Anesthesiologists make sure that the patient's body is not overstimulated or injured by a medical procedure and that the patient feels no pain while undergoing this procedure. Traditionally, anesthesiologists deal mainly in the area of surgery. They do, however, also oversee the administration of anesthetics during other medical procedures and if needed, during childbirth.

After reviewing a patient's medical history, the anesthesiologist will determine the best form of anesthesia for the patient. Different medical problems and different kinds of surgery require different kinds of anesthesia. These determinations are based on the anesthesiologist's broad background in medicine, which includes an understanding of surgical procedures, physiology, pharmacology, and critical care.

In the operating room, an anesthesiologist gives the patient an anesthetic, making them unconscious and numb to pain. This involves administering drugs to put the patient under and maintaining the anesthesia. In some cases, only a regional anesthesia is required—numbing only the part of the body on which the surgery is being performed. In more complex cases, anesthesiologists may need to prepare special equipment such as blood warming devices. Anesthesiologists use monitoring equipment, and insert intravenous lines and breathing tubes. They make sure the mask is secure and allows for a proper airway. In an emergency situation, an anesthesiologist is also part of the cardiopulmonary resuscitation team.

An anesthesiologist pays close attention to the patient's well-being by monitoring blood pressure, breathing, heart rate, and body temperature throughout surgery. It is also the anesthesiologist's responsibility to position the patient properly, so that the doctor can perform the surgery and the patient remains uninjured. The anesthesiologist will also control the patient's temperature, cooling or heating different parts of the body during surgery.

Anesthesiologists are not limited to the operating room; they also spend time with patients before and after surgery. When meeting the patient beforehand, an anesthesiologist explains the kind of anesthesia to be used as well as answers any questions. This interaction is sometimes necessary to put the patient at ease and it also allows the anesthesiologist to get to know the patient before surgery. Unlike other doctors, anesthesiologists do not have the opportunity to work closely for long periods of time with patients.

Anesthesiologists may specialize in a variety of different areas, such as pediatric anesthesia, respiratory therapy, critical care, and cardiovascular anesthesia. This team may consist of anesthesiology residents, nurse anesthetists, and anesthesiology assistants. The anesthesiologist will delegate responsibilities to other members of the care team.

While emergency cases require anesthesiologists to make quick decisions and act without hesitation, in other cases they have time to carefully plan, to study a patient's medical history, to meet with the surgeons and the patients, and to work by a regular schedule. Most anesthesiologists work in hospitals, though they may actually be part of an individual or group practice. Others direct residents in teaching hospitals or teach at medical schools.

Requirements

Postsecondary Training

Students must first earn an M.D. degree and pass an examination to become licensed to practice medicine. (See *Physicians*) Then begins a four-year residency. The first year is spent training in an area of clinical medicine other than anesthesia, such as internal or emergency medicine, pediatrics, surgery, obstetrics, or neurology. The final three years of study are then spent in an anesthesiology residency program accredited by the Accreditation Council for Graduate Medical Education. You can find these accredited residency programs listed in the *Directory of Graduate Medical Education Programs.*

Certification or Licensing

Anesthesiologists receive certification from the American Board of Anesthesiology. In addition to the license, the board requires applicants to have completed training in an accredited program, and to pass an exam. Applicants must also have a Certificate of Clinical Competence. This certificate, filed by the residency training program, attests to the applicant's clinical competence.

Other Requirements

Every surgery calls on an anesthesiologist's ability to pay careful attention and to remain alert. An anesthesiologist sometimes encounters emergency situations, requiring quick, clear-headed responses. But the work can also be slower paced and require patience to comfort people preparing for surgery. Not only must anesthesiologists be able to explain the surgery clearly to patients, but they must be able to direct other members of the anesthesia team.

Earnings

Salaries for anesthesiologists vary according to the kind of practice (whether the anesthesiologist works individually or as part of a group practice), the amount of overhead required to maintain the business, and geographic location. Though working fewer hours, an anesthesiologist can make as much as other doctors. According to a 1998 survey conducted by the American Medical Association, the average net pay for an anesthesiologist is about $228,400 per year, but salaries may range from $171,500 to $268,984.

Fringe benefits for physicians typically include health and dental insurance, paid vacations, and retirement plans.

Outlook

According to the *Occupational Outlook Handbook,* anesthesiology is growing faster than the average. Attracted by the technological advancements, the regularity of the work, and the fewer hours, more people are entering the field. Most anesthesiologists find work immediately after finishing their residencies. As medical advances allow for different kinds of treatment facilities, anesthesiologists will find more work outside of a traditional hospital setting. The development of more outpatient clinics, freestanding surgical centers, and respiratory therapy clinics has opened up employment opportunities for anesthesiologists.

Managed care organizations have changed the way medicine is practiced and may continue to do so. Because anesthesiology is a hospital-based specialty, anesthesiologists must find ways to work within the guidelines of managed care, sometimes to the detriment of medical treatment. Anesthesiologists and other health care professionals will continue to challenge these organizations in order to practice medicine to the best of their abilities.

For More Information

Following are organizations that provide information about a career as an anesthesiologist:

American Board of Anesthesiology
4101 Lake Bonne Trail, Suite 510
Raleigh, NC 27607-7506
Tel: 919-881-2570
Web: http://anesthes.uthscsa.edu/education/address.html

American Society of Anesthesiologists
520 North Northwest Highway
Park Ridge, IL 60068
Tel: 847-825-5586
Web: http://www.asahq.org

Cardiologists

School Subjects
| Biology
| Health

Personal Skills
| Helping/teaching
| Technical/scientific

Work Environment
| Primarily indoors
| Primarily multiple locations

Minimum Education Level
| Medical degree

Salary Range
| $44,400 to $160,000 to $250,000

Certification or Licensing
| Required by all states

Outlook
| Faster than the average

Overview

Cardiologists are physicians who practice in the subspecialty of internal medicine that concentrates on the diagnosis and treatment of heart disease. In most instances, cardiologists treat patients on a consultative basis to determine if the symptoms the patients are exhibiting are signs of heart disease.

History

In 1749, cardiology became a medical specialty when Jean Baptiste Senac published a comprehensive study of the heart. The development of modern cardiology heightened in 1816 when Rene Laennec invented the stethoscope. By the middle of the 19th century, the stethoscope was refined and routinely used as a diagnostic tool for the heart. Further developments, such as Carlo Matteucci's illustrated discovery of the heart's electrical charge in 1838 and Willem Einthoven's modification of the string galvanometer used to record the electrical impulses of the heart in 1903, led to the beginning stages of electrocardiography. Einthoven later refined his device and invented the electrocardiograph, an achievement which won him the Nobel Prize in 1924. Werner Forssman, Dickinson Richards, and Andre F. Cournand also won the Nobel Prize in 1956 for their use of the catheter to study the circulatory system and the heart. This achievement was made possible because of Forssman's earlier invention of the cardiac catheterization technique.

During the latter half of the 20th century, cardiology was marked by advancements in heart surgery. The first heart transplant was performed by Christiaan Barnard in 1967, while the first artificial heart was used in 1982 by a team at the University of Utah.

The Job

During their initial interview, cardiologists review the patient's medical history. After taking the medical history, cardiologists will then perform a physical examination. This is their first opportunity to listen to the patient's heart. Often, a cardiologist can tell if there is a cardiac problem by just listening to the rhythm of the heartbeat. For example, when examining a patient for a heart murmur (an abnormal heartbeat), cardiologists will be able to tell if it is an innocent murmur, or whether it could cause problems.

If warranted, cardiologists will send their patients for specific tests that will aid in their evaluation and diagnosis. The most common test is the electrocardiogram (ECG or EKG). An ECG measures the electrical activity produced by heart contractions and outputs a graph illustrating this. Many problems can be detected through ECGs.

Cardiac catheterization is another type of test. A small tube is inserted through a blood vessel into or near the heart. This procedure is used to take pictures of the heart, which cardiologists can use for diagnosis as well as to evaluate the body's electrical system and in some cases, to remove obstructions.

Another form of test is the echocardiogram. During this procedure, high-pitched sounds, inaudible to the human ear, are sent into the body. Their echoes are plotted by a transducer to create a picture of the heart. A stress echocardiogram evaluates the heart to measure the supply of blood going to the muscles before and after exercise.

Cardiologists do not perform heart surgery; that is done by *thoracic surgeons*. Many surgeons, however, often request cardiologists to consult in the pre-operative phase of treatment.

Also, cardiologists will often provide information and advice to their patients regarding the prevention of cardiac disease. Unfortunately, many of the patients who see cardiologists are advanced in age and find it difficult to change their lifestyles.

Requirements

Postsecondary Training

Once you receive your M.D. degree and become licensed to practice medicine (See *Physicians*), you must take seven to eight more years of additional training. This includes an internship that may last from one to two years and a six-year residency program. Cardiologists spend three years in a residency program in internal medicine and another three years in a residency program in the subspecialty of cardiology.

Certification or Licensing

Cardiologists should be board certified by the American Board of Internal Medicine (ABIM) in both internal medicine and then in the cardiology subspecialty. To be certified in internal medicine, you need to have completed medical school and at least three years of additional training as well as pass a comprehensive exam. Certification in cardiology requires at least three more years of accredited training (in cardiology), proven clinical competence, and passing another comprehensive exam. In 1990 the ABIM began issuing certificates that carried time limitations. This was done to ensure that all certified doctors maintain a high level of competency. For continuing medical education, cardiologists can attend conferences, lectures, or specialized readings.

Other Requirements

Many cardiologists choose to become members of the American College of Cardiology. Membership is a sign of a high level of professionalism and competence. To be considered for various levels of membership, the College takes into account the physician's length of service, board certifications, and scientific accomplishments. The highest level, Fellow, allows the use of the initials F.A.C.C. (Fellow of the American College of Cardiology).

Cardiologists need a nurturing personality. The needs of the patient must always come before their own needs. Cardiologists must be willing to put aside their own concerns while they are responsible for the care of a patient.

Earnings

According to a 1998 survey conducted by the American Medical Association, the mean net income for internal medicine physicians is roughly $185,700, but salaries may begin around $116,306. Cardiologists can expect a higher income considering it is a subspecialty of internal medicine and demands a higher level of training.

Outlook

The influence of managed care is being felt in the field of cardiology. The usual inpatient time for someone who has suffered a heart attack has been greatly reduced. Years ago it was common for heart attack patients to remain in the hospital for a month. However, inpatient hospital time has been steadily decreasing. Today it is not uncommon for a patient to stay in the hospital only five days, and sometimes just two.

Another effect of managed care is that before its introduction, it was not unusual for a patient with chest pain to automatically have an angiogram. Angiograms are very expensive, however, and doctors do not prescribe them as quickly as before.

Another influence on cardiology is the constant research that is being performed in the field. With the influx of new information, the field is continually evolving. According to the *Occupational Outlook Handbook*, physicians' jobs are expected to grow faster than the average through the year 2006.

For More Information

Following are organizations that provide information on the field of cardiology and possible sources of certification information:

American Board of Internal Medicine
510 Walnut Street, Suite 1700
Philadelphia, PA 19106-3699
Tel: 800-441-ABIM
Web: http://www.abim.org

American College of Cardiology
9111 Old Georgetown Road
Bethesda, MD 20814
Tel: 800-253-4636 ext. 630
Web: http://www.acc.org

Dentists

School Subjects	Chemistry Health
Personal Skills	Helping/teaching Technical/scientific
Work Environment	Primarily indoors Primarily one location
Minimum Education Level	Medical degree
Salary Range	$75,000 to $120,000 to $192,000
Certification or Licensing	Required by all states
Outlook	Little change or more slowly than the average

Overview

Dentists attempt to maintain their clients' teeth through such preventive and reparative practices as extracting, filling, cleaning, or replacing teeth. They perform corrective work, such as straightening teeth, and treat diseased tissue of the gums. They also perform surgical operations on the jaw or mouth, and make and fit false teeth.

History

For centuries, the practice of dentistry consisted largely of curing toothaches by extraction or the use of herbs and similar methods to alleviate pain. It was practiced not only by dentists but by barbers and blacksmiths as well. Dental care and correction have become a sophisticated branch of medicine, and dentists are now highly trained professionals of great importance to the public health.

The Job

Most dentists are general practitioners, but almost 20 percent practice as specialists. The largest number of these specialists are orthodontists, followed by oral surgeons, pedodontists, periodontists, prosthodontists, endodontists, oral pathologists, and public health dentists.

General practitioners must be proficient in many areas of dentistry. They not only must handle routine treatments, such as cleaning teeth, extracting teeth, and filling cavities, but must also be on the alert for any condition in the mouth requiring special treatment, such as crooked teeth, diseased gums, and oral cancer. General practitioners must be able to use and understand X rays and be well acquainted with laboratory work.

Specialists devote their time and skills to specific dental problems. *Orthodontists* correct irregularities in the development of teeth and jaws by means of braces and similar devices. *Oral surgeons* perform difficult tooth extractions, remove tumors from the gums or jaw, and set jaw fractures. *Pedodontists* specialize in the care and treatment of children's teeth. *Periodontists* treat diseased gums and other tissues that support the teeth. *Prosthodontists* design, construct, and fit dental prosthetics. *Endodontists* specialize in diseases of the tooth pulp. *Oral pathologists* examine and diagnose tumors and lesions of the mouth. *Public health dentists* work through public health agencies to treat and educate the public on the importance of dental health and care.

Requirements

High School

A high school diploma is required for admission into dental school. In high school, the prospective dental student should be sure to study biology, chemistry, physics, health, and mathematics. Liberal arts courses are also important for meeting college entrance requirements and developing good communications skills. Participation in extracurricular activities is helpful because it provides opportunities to interact with many different people and develop interpersonal skills.

Postsecondary Training

The dental profession is selective, and standards are high. College grades and the amount of college education are carefully considered in the application evaluation process. All dental schools approved by the American Dental Association require applicants to pass the Dental Admissions Test, which gauges a student's prospects of success or failure in dental school. Information on tests and testing centers may be obtained from the Council on Dental Education of the American Dental Association.

Dental schools require at least two years of college-level predental education. About 80 percent of students entering dental schools have already earned a bachelor's or master's degree. Professional training in a dental school generally requires four academic years. Many dental schools have an interdisciplinary curriculum in which the dental student studies basic science with students of medicine, pharmacy, and other health professions. Clinical training is frequently begun in the second year. Most schools now feature a department of community dentistry, which involves a study of communities, urban problems, and sociology, and includes treatment of patients from the community. Generally the degree of doctor of dental surgery (D.D.S.) is granted upon graduation, although some schools give the degree of doctor of dental medicine (D.D.M. or D.M.D.).

Dental students who wish to enter a specialized field should plan on postgraduate study ranging from two to five years. A specialist can only become certified by passing specialty board exams. A dentist may obtain further training as a dental intern or resident in an approved hospital. Dentists must continually keep abreast of developments in the profession through reading professional magazines and journals, taking short-term graduate courses, and participating in seminars.

Certification or Licensing

All 50 states and the District of Columbia require dentists to be licensed. To qualify for a license in most states, a candidate must graduate from a dental school accredited by the American Dental Association's Commission on Dental Accreditation and pass written and practical examinations. Candidates may fulfill the written part of the exam by passing the National Board Dental Examinations. Individual states or regional testing agencies give the written or practical examinations. Generally, dentists licensed in one state are required to take another exam to practice in another state. However, 20 states grant licenses to dentists from other states based on their credentials.

Other Requirements

Manual dexterity and scientific ability are important. Skilled, steady hands are necessary, as are good spatial judgment and some artistic ability. Good vision is required because of the detailed work.

Exploring

You might be able to gain an awareness of the demands of dentistry by observing a dentist at work. Work as a dental hygienist, dental assistant, or dental laboratory technician might lead to continued study in dentistry. Because of the nature of dentistry, developing good manual dexterity through sculpting or metalworking would be helpful to the prospective dentist.

Employers

Most dentists are in private practice, either on their own or in a group practice. Other opportunities for dentists can be found in such arenas as the armed forces, public health services, hospitals, and clinics, for example.

Starting Out

Once a dentist has graduated from an approved dental school and passed a state licensing examination, there are three common avenues of entry into private practice. A dentist may open a new office, purchase an established practice, or join another dentist or group of dentists to gain further experience. There are, however, other choices for licensed dentists. They may enter the armed forces as commissioned officers, or, through civil service procedures, become eligible for work in the U.S. Public Health Service. They may also choose to work in hospitals, clinics, or schools. For some, work in the dental laboratory or in teaching dentistry will provide a satisfying career.

Advancement

Advancement for the newly licensed dentist in private practice depends on personal skill in handling patients as well as dental work. Through the years, the successful dentist builds a reputation and thus advances with a growing clientele. The quality of the work depends in part on an ability to keep up with developments in the field. For salaried dentists in the various areas of employment, advancement will also depend on the quality and skill of their work. Advancement may take the form of a step from general practitioner to specialist, a step requiring further study and generally providing higher income. Teachers may look forward to administrative positions or to appointments as professors.

Success may also depend on the location of the practice; people in higher-income areas are more likely to request dental care. In small towns and sparsely populated areas a great need exists for dentists, and competition is slight. In cities where there are many dentists, it may be more difficult to establish a practice despite the larger pool of possible patients.

Earnings

Beginning dentists, faced with the expense of buying equipment and the problem of establishing a practice, generally earn enough to cover expenses and little more. However, income rises rapidly as the dentist's practice becomes established. According to the American Dental Association, the average net income of self-employed dentists is about $120,000 a year; specialists averaged $192,000.

Dentists' earnings are lower during economic downturns when people tend to postpone dental treatment except for emergencies.

Work Environment

Because most dentists are in private practice, they are free to set their hours and establish offices and atmospheres suitable to their individual tastes. Most dentists work from 4 to 5 days a week, many times averaging 40 or more hours. They spend about 89 percent of their time treating patients. The beginning dentist must set aside expensive decorating plans in favor of suitable equipment, but most dentists' offices are designed to be pleasant and comfortable. Dentists may have dental assistants, hygienists, or laboratory technicians, or they may carry out the special duties of each themselves. However, there is a growing trend to leave simpler tasks, teeth cleaning for example, to dental assistants and hygienists, so dentists have more time to perform higher-paying procedures, such as root canals.

The dentist in private practice sets individual hours and practices after office hours only in emergencies. Salaried dentists working for a clinic, hospital, or the Public Health Service are subject to conditions set by their employers.

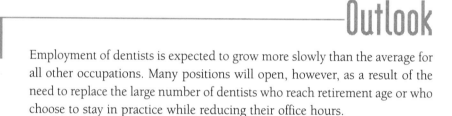

Outlook

Employment of dentists is expected to grow more slowly than the average for all other occupations. Many positions will open, however, as a result of the need to replace the large number of dentists who reach retirement age or who choose to stay in practice while reducing their office hours.

Additionally, opportunities for specialists, such as cosmetic dentists, will be very good through the year 2006. That specialty was listed in *US News & World Report* as one of the best jobs for the future. Three-fourths of American adults believe that a winning smile is related to job success. Most adults are unhappy with their teeth, creating a demand for dentists skilled in cosmetic techniques such as bleaching and veneering. People are concerned about dental health and can usually afford dental care, especially as dental insurance becomes more readily available. Cosmetic dentists will be in demand in large metropolitan areas such as Los Angeles and Chicago.

Scientific advances in the field offer a promising future for specialists. The work of the oral pathologist or orthodontist, for example, will increase as people become more aware of the need for such care. Public health programs, too, can be expected to expand. Dentistry today is focusing more on preventive care than reparative practice.

Interestingly, even though the number of applicants to dental schools is decreasing, standards remain high and admission is competitive. The number of women graduating from dental schools is increasing. High school students must be aware of the importance of maintaining high grades if they wish to qualify. Despite diminishing enrollments, the number of new graduates entering the field each year is larger than the number of openings. Dentists rarely leave the profession except to retire, and many continue to work beyond retirement age, simply reducing the number of hours they work.

There were 162,000 dentists employed in the United States in 1996. Nine out of 10 were in private practice. Of the remainder, about half worked in research or teaching, or held administrative positions in dental schools. Some practiced in hospitals and clinics. About 79 percent of all dentists were general practitioners; the rest were specialists.

The expense of pursuing an education in dentistry and setting up a practice is significant. The prospective dental student should be aware of these financial demands before entering the field. However, in a recent survey reported in the magazine *Inc.*, dental offices were the third highest ranking category of start-up businesses most likely to survive. According to the American Dental Association, among dentists out of dental school less than four years, about 42 percent owned their practice; by six years after graduation, 53 percent had their own practices.

For More Information

For information on admission requirements of U.S. and Canadian dental schools, contact:

American Association of Dental Schools
1625 Massachusetts Avenue, NW, Suite 600
Washington, DC 20036
Tel: 202-667-9433
Email: aada@aada.jhu.edu
Web: http://www.aads.jhu.edu/

For a list of accredited schools for postgraduate and postdoctoral work, contact:

American Dental Association
Department of Career Guidance
211 East Chicago Avenue
Chicago, IL 60611
Tel: 312-440-2500
Web: http://www.ada.org/tc-educ.html

For information on careers in dentistry, visit this Web site:

So you want to be a dentist?
Web: http://www.vvm.com/~bond/home.htm

Dermatologists

Overview

Dermatologists study, diagnose, and treat diseases and ailments of the skin, hair, mucous membranes, nails, and related tissues or structures. They may also perform cosmetic services, such as scar removal or hair transplants.

History

Many in the medical profession opposed specialization when it began to occur in the 19th century. They thought treatments would be too fragmented for patients' own good. There were several factors, however, that made specialization inevitable. The amount of medical information was increasing and complex new techniques were developing at such a rapid pace that doctors could not keep up with the advances. They began to send patients to physicians who concentrated on one type of illness or manipulation.

Specialization was also attractive because it gave doctors the opportunity to demand higher fees, work fewer hours, and command greater respect from peers and the public. Medical experts gradually abandoned their ideas that general disease was caused by humoral problems and began to diagnose and treat local organs instead.

The specialty of dermatology had its beginnings in the mid-1800s in Vienna when a doctor named Ferdinand von Hebra, one of the first to specialize entirely in skin diseases, founded a division of dermatology. At that time, medicine concentrated primarily on abnormalities in the four humors, or elemental fluids of the body—blood, phlegm, black bile, and yellow bile—and they believed symptoms were caused by those abnormalities. Hebra made classifications based on changes in the tissues instead of on symptoms or on general disease categories. As a result, his treatment was directed toward the local problem rather than treating imbalances in the humors. He was responsible for the discovery that scabies was transmissible from person to person and could be cured by the destruction of the itch-mite parasite.

Dermatologists use magnifying lenses to view the skin up close. Innumerable discoveries have been made, including new medicines, treatments, and equipment. Lasers and computer technology, for example, have drastically changed dermatology, improving diagnostic techniques and allowing certain surgical procedures to be performed without using a scalpel.

The Job

Dermatologists study, diagnose, and treat diseases and ailments of the largest, most visible organ of the body, the skin, and its related tissues and structures—hair, mucous membranes, and nails. Their work begins with diagnosis to determine the cause of the disease or condition. This process involves studying a patient's history, conducting visual examinations, and taking blood samples, smears of the affected skin, microscopic scrapings, or biopsy specimens of the skin. They may order cultures of fungi or bacteria, or perform patch and photosensitivity tests to reveal allergies and immunologic diseases. They may also evaluate bone marrow, lymph nodes, and endocrine glands. Usually dermatologists send skin, tissue, or blood specimens to a laboratory for chemical and biological testing and analysis.

Dermatologists treat some skin problems with prescribed oral medications, such as antibiotics, or topical applications. Certain types of eczema and dermatitis, psoriasis, acne, or impetigo can usually be treated with creams, ointments, or oral medicines.

Exposure to ultraviolet light is used to treat such conditions as psoriasis, and radiation therapy is occasionally used to treat keloids (scar tissue that grows excessively).

Some skin conditions and illnesses require surgical treatment. There are three types of skin cancer—basal cell carcinoma, squamous cell carcinoma, and malignant melanoma—which must be removed surgically. Dermatologists may use traditional surgery, where the cancerous cells and surrounding tissue are cut away, but some cancers can be removed by lasers, frozen by cryosurgery, destroyed with a cautery device (high-frequency electric current), or destroyed by radiation therapy. Another type of surgery dermatologists use is Moh's surgery, in which progressive layers of skin and tissue are cut out and examined microscopically for the presence of cancers. Dermatologists also perform skin graft procedures to repair wounds that are too large to be stitched together. After removal of a skin tumor, for example, they take a portion of skin from another part of the patient's body, such as the thigh, and attach it to the wound. Since the skin graft comes from the patient's own body, there is no problem with rejection.

Not all surgeries that dermatologists perform are major. There are many conditions that can be treated with simple outpatient procedures under local anesthetic, including removal of warts, sebaceous cysts, scars, moles, cosmetic defects of the skin, boils, and abscesses. Hair transplants are usually done in the doctor's office, as are laser treatments for disfiguring birth defects, cysts, birthmarks, spider veins, and growths.

Certain diseases can manifest themselves in a skin condition. When dermatologists see that a skin problem is a sign of an illness in another part of the patient's body, they recommend treatment by other specialists. If a patient complains of itchy or scaly skin, for example, it may be an allergy. Boils may be a sign of diabetes mellitus, and a skin rash may indicate secondary syphilis. Dermatologists must often consult with allergists, internists, and other doctors. In turn, many dermatologists are called on by other specialists to help diagnose complicated symptoms.

Dermatologists not only deal with the physical aspects of skin afflictions, but the emotional aspects, too. Patients often have to face embarrassment, ridicule, and rejection because of their skin ailments, and dermatologists can help them overcome this kind of trauma.

Within the field of dermatology there are some subspecialties. *Dermatoimmunologists* focus on the treatment of diseases that involve the immune system, including allergies. They may use a procedure called immunofluorescence to diagnose and characterize these skin disorders.

Dermatopathologists study the tissue structure and features of skin diseases. *Dermatologic surgeons* perform Moh's micrographic surgery and cosmetic procedures, including collagen injections, sclerotherapy (the injection of varicose veins with a fluid), and dermabrasion (a planing of the skin using sandpaper, wire brushes, or other abrasive materials). *Pediatric dermatologists* treat skin disorders in children. *Occupational dermatologists* study and treat occupational disorders, such as forms of dermatitis from chemical or biological irritants.

Some dermatologists combine a private practice with a teaching position at a medical school. Others are involved in research, developing new treatments, and finding cures for skin ailments. A few work in industry, developing cosmetics, lotions, and other consumer products.

Requirements

High School

High school classes that can prepare you for medical studies include physics, biology, anatomy, and chemistry. Courses in English, other humanities, mathematics, and the social sciences will also provide a useful background for your undergraduate work.

Postsecondary Training

Those interested in a career in dermatology must first earn an M.D. degree (See *Physicians*). Then physicians begin their residencies. Only about half of the applicants for the 100 accredited residency programs in the United States are accepted, and dermatology is very competitive.

Medical school and the dermatological residency are filled with stress and pressure, and they are also physically demanding. Residents often work 24-hour shifts and put in 80 hours a week or more. Physicians need emotional stability and the ability to make decisions on critical medical issues. They must have keen observation skills, be detail oriented, and also be able to relate to people with compassion and understanding.

The American Board of Dermatology, an organization that certifies dermatologists, requires four years of residency training, three of which must be training in dermatology. The first year is a clinical residency program in internal medicine, family practice, general surgery, or pediatrics. The next three years are spent studying and practicing dermatology. Residents are closely supervised as they study skin pathology, bacteriology, radiology, surgery, biochemistry, allergy and immunology, and other basics. Intensive laboratory work in mycology (the study of the fungi that infect humans) is usually required.

Certification or Licensing

Although licensing is required to practice medicine, certification by the dermatological governing board is voluntary and affirms that dermatologists are qualified to practice this specialty. The American Board of Dermatology administers written and sometimes practical examinations and certifies those who meet the standards for practice. Certification is for a period of ten years. Even after 11 years of study, dermatologists must continue to study throughout their careers in order to keep up with medical advances and retain board certification.

Exploring

Students interested in a career in medicine can visit hospitals, clinics, and health care facilities. Those specifically interested in dermatology can visit dermatologic offices. Students should also consider volunteering at a hospital or clinic where they will gain experience working in a health care setting and be exposed to a variety of medical specialties. Your doctor may also have suggestions for how to explore this medical field.

Employers

Most dermatologists are in private practice, either individually or with others. A few work for hospitals or similar health agencies. Some establish their practices at large university medical centers in order to combine an active practice with teaching at a university or medical school. Researchers work in university or private laboratories searching for new cures and treatments.

Starting Out

Once a doctor finishes the residency program, there are several options for beginning to practice dermatology. The most difficult is to set up a private practice. It is a considerable expense to purchase the necessary equipment and supplies, pay staff salaries, rent office space, pay liability insurance, and advertise. It can take up to 15 years to become established and reach full earning potential.

A second option is to take over the practice of a dermatologist who is retiring or relocating. This has the benefit of offering an already existing patient list.

Some dermatologists join a group practice or enter into partnership with a related medical specialist such as an allergist, an immunologist, or a plastic surgeon.

Many newly qualified dermatologists are much more likely to take salaried jobs in group medical practices, clinics, or health maintenance organizations. After several years, they may decide to open their own practice. Some find opportunities with federal or state agencies, private businesses, or the military.

Advancement

Dermatologists with their own private practices can increase their earnings or improve their clinical status by expanding their practices or moving to larger cities. They may become teachers at medical schools in addition to treating patients, or they may go into research.

Some go into hospital administration, where they have less contact with patients and more involvement with staff and the day-to-day operation of the hospital.

Many physicians participate in national organizations—such as the American Medical Association or the American Academy of Dermatology—where they can serve on committees and be elected to offices, increasing their status.

Earnings

Physicians begin to earn a salary when they start their residencies. In the first year, they average $32,800, and the salary increases to $40,800 by their last year. The amount varies with the kind of residency, the hospital, and the geographic area.

A survey of physicians conducted by the Hay Group, a management consultancy, showed dermatologists averaging $166,500 per year. This is slightly lower than average for all physicians. The American Medical Association reports that the average earnings for physicians who had their own practice was $200,000 a year in 1996. These earnings vary with the subspecialty, the number of years in practice, geographic region, hours worked, and the skill, personality, and professional standing of the specialist.

Beginning dermatologists can expect to earn $80,000, while experienced dermatologists with their own practices or full partnerships in a group practice can earn over $200,000. Average salaries are $115,000 to $238,000.

Dermatologists in private practice or group partnerships have the potential for higher earnings, but they must cover all of their own business expenses and benefits. For those hired by health care organizations, in addition to salary, dermatologists may receive benefits, including health and life insurance, malpractice liability insurance, paid vacation, and retirement plans. Some earn productivity bonuses as well.

Work Environment

Dermatologists are often solo practitioners. They work in well-lighted, air-conditioned offices, and they are usually assisted by clerical and nursing staff. A certain number of hours are spent each week visiting patients at the hospital. Most dermatologists also spend some time in laboratory settings, either their own or in a hospital. Most specialists, including dermatologists, work in large urban areas.

Working hours are usually regular, since dermatologists see patients by appointment in their offices. They schedule surgeries and follow-up visits both at their offices and at hospitals. Dermatologists occasionally may have to answer emergency calls, such as to treat burn victims.

Dermatologists work 40 to 50 hours a week, mostly during normal daytime hours, though some work up to 60 hours a week. They often try to accommodate the working schedules of their patients by opening their offices on Saturdays or one evening a week.

Outlook

The health care industry is thriving, and the employment of physicians is expected to grow faster than the average for all occupations through the year 2006. According to the American Academy of Dermatology, there are over 11,000 practicing dermatologists in the United States and Canada. Approximately 1.2 percent of all physicians are dermatologists.

New technologies, medicines, and treatments continue to be developed at a rapid pace. Another factor in the growth of this industry is that the population is growing and aging, requiring more health care in advancing years. Demand for dermatologists has increased as people have become aware of the effects of radiation exposure from the sun and of air pollutants on skin. The public is also much more aware of the benefits of good general and dermatological health.

New physicians will be more likely to choose salaried positions in hospitals, clinics, and health maintenance organizations, opting for regular work hours and the opportunity for peer consultation.

For More Information

The AAD can give you good medical information on dermatological conditions as well as employment opportunities and professional concerns:

American Academy of Dermatology
930 North Meacham Road
Schaumburg, IL 60168-4014
Tel: 847-330-0230 or 888-462-DERM
Web: http://www.aad.org

Consult the American Board of Dermatology for everything you need to know about certification, plus a lot more—and virtually all of it is available online:

American Board of Dermatology
Henry Ford Hospital
1 Ford Place
Detroit, MI 48202-3450
Tel: 313-874-1088
Web: http://www.abderm.org

Ear, Nose, and Throat Specialists

School Subjects
Biology
Health

Personal Skills
Helping/teaching
Technical/scientific

Work Environment
Primarily indoors
Primarily multiple locations

Minimum Education Level
Medical degree

Salary Range
$44,400 to $160,000 to $250,000

Certification or Licensing
Required by all states

Outlook
Faster than the average

Overview

An *ear, nose, and throat (ENT) specialist,* or *otolaryngologist,* provides comprehensive medical and surgical care for patients with diseases and disorders that involve or affect the ears, nose, throat, and related structures of the head and neck. Fifty percent of all physician office visits are for ear, nose, and throat illnesses. Many ENT specialists operate in private practices or work in large academic/university settings where they help train medical students and residents. In 1996, there were approximately 9,000 ENT specialists.

History

Ear, nose, and throat, or otolaryngology, is the oldest medical specialty in the United States. This specialty manages diseases of the ears, nose, nasal passages, sinuses, larynx (voice box), and oral cavity and upper pharynx (mouth and throat) as well as structures of the neck and face.

The Job

Ear, nose, and throat specialists deal with problems as varied as adenoid infections, allergies, ear aches, earwax buildup, hay fever, snoring, and many far more serious conditions or diseases such as throat cancer. The expertise of the ENT specialist involves knowledge of more than nine other medical disciplines including neurosurgery (skull base disorders), plastic and reconstructive surgery, ophthalmology (abnormalities near the eye), oral surgery, allergy, dermatology (skin disorders), oncology (head and neck cancer), and pediatrics and family practice. The ENT specialist usually sees patients in a clinic or office setting to evaluate symptoms that affect their ears, nose, throat, and related structures of the head and neck. Otolaryngologists work closely with other physicians, sometimes referring patients to other specialists. Frequently they work with other medical specialties to solve single or multiple medical issues or to perform extensive surgery. For instance, some ENT specialists may be trained to perform reconstructive surgery using skin flaps or grafts to close a hole created by the removal of a tumor. Other surgical procedures, such as a cochlear implant, may help a patient regain some hearing and be able to communicate better with the world.

Requirements

Postsecondary Training

After receiving the medical degree and becoming licensed to practice medicine (See *Physicians*), medical students who have decided to go into otolaryngology are required to complete two years of study in general surgery as their internship. Then they enter a three-year residency program in otolaryngology—head and neck surgery. At the end of the five-year postgraduate training, an ENT specialist who wants to subspecialize completes additional training through fellowships.

Certification or Licensing

The American Board of Otolaryngology (ABOto) certifies physicians in otolaryngology and its subspecialty fields. In order to be a candidate for certification in otolaryngology, a physician must have successfully completed medical school and five years of required graduate specialty training. The certification requires passing a two-part examination.

Other Requirements

To be a successful ENT specialist, you should be a good clinician, pay close attention to detail, and have good hand-eye coordination and manual dexterity. Other important attributes include being a good listener and having good communication skills. You should also enjoy working with people and respect your patients. Being imaginative and adaptable is also a good trait for this profession.

Earnings

Generally, the median income for various medical specialties according to 1995 American Medical Association figures ranges from $124,000 to $230,000. There are no income figures specific to ENT specialists.

Outlook

The expertise of the ENT specialist will always be in great demand and as the population ages, their skills may be more valuable. Overall, the health care industry is thriving and the employment of physicians in almost all fields is expected to grow faster than the average through 2006.

For More Information

The following organizations provide information on the profession of ENT specialists.

American Academy of Otolaryngology—Head and Neck Surgery
One Price Street
Alexandria, VA 22314
Tel: 703-836-4444
Web: http://www.entnet.org

American College of Surgeons
633 North Saint Clair Street
Chicago, IL 60611
Tel: 312-202-5000
Web: http://www.facs.org/

American Society for Head and Neck Surgery
203 Lathrop Street, Suite 519
Pittsburgh, PA 15213
Tel: 412-647-2227
Web: http://www.usassociations.com/ashns

Endodontists

Overview

Endodontists are dental specialists who diagnose and treat diseases of the dental pulp and root. They perform root canal treatment, often handling cases that are too complicated for a general dentist. Endodontists also treat oral trauma, managing teeth that have been cracked or broken, knocked out, twisted in the socket, or pushed further into the tooth socket.

History

Although the endodontic specialty is relatively new, endodontic procedures have been performed for more than 2,000 years. A skull dating back to the second or third century BC was found in a desert in Israel; one tooth contained a bronze wire that may have been used to treat an infected pulp.

Before the modern era, dentists cauterized the pulp or covered it with protective coatings such as gold foil. In the early 19th century, dentists attempted to kill the nerves in the pulp by applying arsenic and morphine.

Twentieth-century advances in endodontics included X rays for diagnosis, electric pulp testers to determine whether a pulp is dead, and antiseptics to eliminate bacteria in the root canal. Effective anesthesia also has allowed dentists to make root canal treatment more comfortable for the patient.

In the present day, endodontists take advantage of many technological advances. They may use ultrasonic files to clean out the root canal. New combinations of metals, such as nickel-titanium alloys, are used to make endodontic files. Digital radiography offers immediate viewing of X-ray images on computer screens and exposes patients to a lower radiation dose.

The Job

Endodontists specialize in diagnosing and treating diseases of the dental pulp, which consists of nerves, blood vessels, and other cells inside the tooth's root. The primary treatment they provide is commonly known as a "root canal"; what endodontic treatment actually involves is removal of the pulp from within the root canal, followed by filling of the root canal.

Often, endodontic treatment is the only way to save a tooth that would otherwise have to be extracted. While root canal treatment is rumored to be painful, it is the diseased pulp that is painful; root canal treatment eliminates the problem and the pain, and may be the only way to save a tooth from extraction.

Endodontists take X rays of affected teeth to determine what condition could be causing the pain. They also do tests to learn whether the tooth pulp is still vital, or "alive"; they evaluate the tooth's response to temperature changes, electrical stimulation, and tapping.

When performing a root canal, the endodontist anesthetizes the tooth and drills a hole in the tooth to gain access to the pulp chamber. Using small instruments called files, the endodontist cleans and shapes the root canal, removing the pulpal tissue. After the canal has been disinfected, it is obturated, or filled, with substances such as gutta-percha. Obturation is usually performed at a later appointment. The obturated tooth is then restored to function with a crown.

In some cases, endodontic surgery is required. The endodontist cuts through the gum surgically to expose the diseased root and surrounding bone. A portion of the root may be removed surgically.

While general dentists frequently perform routine root canal treatment, endodontists are better equipped to handle more complex cases. When pain is extreme or persists despite routine root canal procedures performed by their general dentist, patients may be referred to an endodontist. Complicated cases involving extra tooth roots, oddly shaped root canals, or calcification also may require a specialist. Patients who need root canal treatment and have serious medical conditions also may be best treated by an endodontic specialist.

Endodontists also treat patients with dental injuries such as oral trauma, cracked or broken teeth, teeth that have been twisted in the socket, and teeth that have been knocked out. Injured teeth often can be saved only by root canal treatment.

Those who manage their own practices must hire, train, and supervise employees, including office staff and dental hygienists.

Requirements

Postsecondary Training

To enter dental school, applicants generally need significant college course work in the sciences, a bachelor's degree, and a good score on the Dental Admissions Test, or DAT. After completing four years of dental school, dentists who want to specialize in endodontics attend a two- to three-year graduate training program.

Certification or Licensing

Before entering practice, dentists must pass a licensing examination. Qualified candidates may also seek certification by the American Board of Endodontics.

Other Requirements

Endodontists, more than most dentists, must have superb hand-eye coordination and the ability to do finely detailed work. As procedures and technology change, practicing endodontists must continue lifelong learning.

They stay up-to-date on advances in their specialty by taking continuing education courses each year. Also, because many dentists own their own practices, knowledge of business practices is beneficial.

Employers

Like general dentists, most endodontists are in private practice. They may have a solo practice or work in a group practice with other dentists. Dentists serving in the military treat members of the military and their families. The U.S. Public Health Service also employs dentists to provide care or conduct research. Endodontists may also teach full time or part time in dental schools. Hospitals employ dentists to treat hospitalized patients.

Starting Out

After completing dental school and an advanced training program in endodontology, most endodontists either start their own practices or join an established practice. While many dentists choose to have their own practices, start-up costs can be steep: new dentists often need to borrow money to buy or lease office space and buy expensive equipment.

Advancement

Endodontists in private practice advance their careers by building their reputation among the general dentists who refer patients to specialists. To establish a good reputation, it is important to communicate effectively and coordinate treatment with general dentists.

Endodontists who teach at dental schools may advance in academic rank and eventually chair the department of endodontology.

Experienced endodontists and endodontic researchers can become more prominent through professional activities such as writing scientific books and articles and being active in professional organizations such as the American Association of Endodontists.

Earnings

According to the American Dental Association Survey Center, endodontists under age 40 have an average net salary of about $154,000. This represents the lower end of the salary range. Endodontists who have been in practice for some time generally have higher earnings; the average net salary for endodontists over age 40 is $178,000.

Salaries also vary by geographic region and are influenced by the number of other endodontists practicing in a community.

Benefits vary by place of employment. Self-employed endodontists often arrange their own benefits through their dental practices.

Work Environment

Most endodontists work in private dental practices. The hours worked vary. Endodontists treat many toothaches on an emergency basis, so they may be on call during the night.

While many dentists wear comfortable business attire underneath a laboratory coat, some opt to wear surgical scrubs when treating patients.

Endodontists may travel from time to time to attend continuing education courses or meetings held by professional organizations.

Outlook

As long as people place a priority on retaining their teeth, endodontists' services will continue to be in demand. The longer life spans of the U.S. population and increasing rates of tooth retention mean that there will be more teeth that require treatment in the future. The emergency nature of many endodontic cases also keeps the demand steady.

Digital radiography is one of the technological advances that are changing the way endodontists practice. Digital radiography allows them to expose patients to less radiation, which is important because endodontists use X rays more than most dentists. Digital radiographs are displayed on computer screens, allowing patients to better understand their condition.

Another development is the use of nickel-titanium files. They are more flexible than the steel files that endodontists have traditionally used to clean root canals.

Endodontists are beginning to use operating microscopes to see better inside the tiny root canal.

For More Information

The following is a professional organization for specialists in endodontics. It sponsors the Journal of Endodontics *and a member newsletter and holds an annual meeting. It has approximately 5,000 members.*

American Association of Endodontists
211 East Chicago Avenue
Chicago, IL 60611-2691
Tel: 312-266-7255
Email: info@aae.org
Web: http://www.aae.org

This primary professional organization for dentists promotes dental health and the dental profession through education, research, and advocacy. It publishes the Journal of the American Dental Association *and* ADA News *and holds an annual conference. It has 120,000 members.*

American Dental Association
Department of Career Guidance
211 East Chicago Avenue
Chicago, IL 60611
Tel: 312-440-2500
Email: publicinfo@ada.org
Web: http://www.ada.org/tc-educ.html

Epidemiologists

School Subjects
Biology
Health

Personal Skills
Helping/teaching
Technical/scientific

Work Environment
Primarily indoors
Primarily multiple locations

Minimum Education Level
Master's degree

Salary Range
$27,000 to $58,000 to $250,000

Certification or Licensing
None available

Outlook
Faster than the average

Overview

Epidemiologists study the cause, spread, and control of diseases affecting groups of people or communities. They use statistics, research, and field investigations to try to connect incidences of a disease with characteristics of populations and communities. Some epidemiologists focus on infectious diseases, which are caused by bacteria and viruses and include AIDS, chicken pox, rabies, and meningitis. Others focus on noninfectious diseases including heart disease, lung cancer, breast cancer, and ulcers.

History

"Epidemiology" comes from the word epidemic, which refers to a disease affecting large numbers of people. This branch of medical science did not become possible until the 1800s, when statistics and statistical analysis were developed. There are some signs, however, that earlier civilizations were making connections between disease and environmental factors. Early

Hippocratic writings connect specific diseases to locations, seasons, and climates. In 1865, Louis Pasteur showed that a specific organism was causing an epidemic in silkworms. Robert Koch, a German bacteriologist, established the bacterial cause of tuberculosis and other diseases in humans in 1882.

Toward the mid-1900s, chronic disease epidemiology began, focusing on the rise in peptic ulcer disease, coronary heart disease, and lung cancer. Chronic disease epidemiologists have helped show the links between smoking and lung cancer.

Today, epidemiologists are increasingly interested in global health patterns and in applying new computer technology to the field.

The Job

Epidemiologists use research, statistical analysis, field investigations, and laboratory techniques to try to figure out the cause of a disease, how it spreads, and what can be done to prevent and control it. They measure the incidence of a disease and relate it to characteristics of populations and environments. Many work on developing new methods or refining old ways of measuring and evaluating incidence of disease.

Epidemiologists' work is important to the medical community and to public health officials, who use their information to determine public health policies. Epidemiologists often develop and recommend public health policies using the research they have collected.

The field of epidemiology is complex. Different epidemiologists focus on different things. *Infectious disease epidemiologists* focus on diseases caused by bacteria and viruses. *Chronic disease epidemiologists* focus on noninfectious diseases that can be genetic. Some epidemiologists have done work on rising teenage suicide rates and murders by guns because they are considered epidemics.

Each state has its own head epidemiologist, who is usually part of the state's public health service. These state epidemiologists work closely with the U.S. Centers for Disease Control and Prevention (CDC) in Atlanta. States are required by law to report certain diseases in their populations to the CDC on a regular basis. For example, states must report outbreaks of influenza or incidences of food poisoning to the CDC.

Requirements

Postsecondary Training

Most epidemiologists have at least a master's degree in public health. To enter a graduate program in epidemiology, the minimum requirement is a bachelor's degree. Undergraduate course work should include biology, chemistry, mathematics, and statistics.

Many graduate programs in epidemiology are geared toward people who already have a medical degree. Most are four-year programs. It is recommended that graduate students pursuing the field of epidemiology get practical experience in the field while they are in school.

Other Requirements

Epidemiologists need to be good scientists and statisticians. They also need to be skilled with computers and like helping people. Curiosity, determination, persistence, and drive will help in research.

Employers

Epidemiologists work for state public health services, local communities, and counties. The CDC employs many epidemiologists, too. Different branches of the CDC focus on different diseases or public-health practices. Epidemiologists with the CDC may conduct research, help states exchange information about disease control and prevention, and help make recommendations for public health policies.

Some epidemiologists work for universities, where they teach and do research. Others work for the World Health Organization (WHO) and the AIDS Institute. Hospitals also employ epidemiologists, usually to research chronic or infectious diseases.

Starting Out

After receiving at least a bachelor's degree, you would be eligible to start a graduate program in epidemiology. Many graduate students in these programs, however, have a medical degree. Typical programs are four years, but there are some two-year degree programs. During graduate school, you should start approaching employers about jobs.

Advancement

Advancement in the field of epidemiology depends on your interest and where you are working. An epidemiologist teaching at a university could advance from assistant professor to full professor. Epidemiologists working for a state's head epidemiologist could move on to become the state epidemiologist there or in another state. Some epidemiologists might want to advance to international work.

Earnings

The salary range for epidemiologists is $27,000 to $58,000 to as high as $250,000. Salaries depend on an epidemiologist's schooling, research, experience, and qualifications.

Work Environment

Depending on where epidemiologists work, part of their day might be spent in the office and part in the community. Most spend part of their time working in teams and part on their own. They may monitor the site of a disease, take samples, collect data, and check out any outbreaks among community residents. Back in the office, they might download their data, conduct research, analyze samples, and write reports.

Outlook

The job outlook for epidemiologists is good. There is an increasing need to understand, control, and prevent the spread of disease around the world. Sometimes, organisms that cause infectious diseases become resistant to vaccines. New diseases or new strains of diseases are discovered all the time. And some diseases, such as AIDS, have no known cure.

For More Information

For information on continuing education and certification, contact:

Association for Professionals in Infection Control and Epidemiology
1275 K Street, NW, Suite 1000
Washington, DC 20005-4006
Tel: 202-789-1890
Fax: 202-789-1899
Web: http://www.apic.org

For publications and training and employment opportunities, contact:

Centers for Disease Control and Prevention
1600 Clifton Road, NE
Atlanta, GA 30333
Tel: 404-639-3311
Web: http://www.cdc.gov

For information on career development and job opportunities, contact:

Infectious Diseases Society of America
99 Canal Center Plaza, Suite 210
Alexandria, VA 22314
Tel: 703-299-0200
Web: http://www.idsociety.org

Gastroenterologists

School Subjects
- Biology
- Health

Personal Skills
- Helping/teaching
- Technical/scientific

Work Environment
- Primarily indoors
- Primarily multiple locations

Minimum Education Level
- Medical degree

Salary Range
- $44,400 to $160,000 to $250,000

Certification or Licensing
- Required by all states

Outlook
- Faster than the average

Overview

Gastroenterologists are physicians who specialize in the treatment of the digestive system and associated organs, like the liver and gall bladder.

History

The field of gastoenterology goes back decades. The American College of Gastroenterology was founded in 1932. The study of the digestive system is as old as medicine, but in recent years there have been a number of important breakthroughs. Peptic ulcers, a common type of ulcer affecting millions of people, have been linked to the Heliobacter pylori bacteria. Through research, gastroenterologists learned that treating patients with antibiotics, along with the regular treatments given for ulcers, dramatically lowered the recurrence of the disease. Other advances are technological. Computers and fiber-optic technology have allowed gastroenterologists tremendous flexibility in the diagnosis and treatment of conditions that in the past would have required surgery. Any disease of the digestive system, from chronic heartburn to cancer, is treated by gastroenterologists.

The Job

Gastroenterologists are internal medicine physicians specializing in the treatment of the digestive system, including the small and large intestines, colon, stomach, esophagus, and liver. They examine patients, prescribe drugs when needed, diagnose disease, and perform various procedures to treat those diseases.

Gastroenterologists work closely with other specialists in treating patients. Oncologists (cancer specialists), cardiologists (heart specialists), and surgeons may cooperate to ensure the best possible care. The chronic nature of many gastrointestinal problems means that doctors often have patients for years, building long-term relationships.

Dr. Peter McNally is the chief of gastroenterology at the Eisenhower Army Medical Center in Augusta, Georgia, where he has practiced since 1996. He is also the chairman of the Public Relations Committee of the American College of Gastroenterology.

Eisenhower Army Medical Center is a major Army hospital in the Southeast. The center is supplied with the latest equipment, which not every hospital can afford, and serves patients referred from several states. "We have a referral base of over one million," says Dr. McNally. "We see the toughest cases.

"Gastroenterology is different from a lot of specialties in that you take a patient all the way through, from start to finish," he says. Technological advances in gastroenterology have made the diagnosis and treatment of certain types of gastrointestinal problems much easier on the patient. One of these advances is endoscopy, the use of lighted, flexible tubes to peer into areas of the body that could only be seen during surgery before. "It's really amazing," Dr. McNally says of endoscopy. "There are forceps and blades eight feet from your hands. You control it all by computer." One procedure making use of endoscopy is polyp removal. A polyp is a kind of growth in the intestines that can become cancerous. "Thirty years ago, when a polyp was found, they would have to resect (perform surgery)," he explains. "Now we can treat the problem sooner and with fewer complications than we could with surgery."

Requirements

Postsecondary Training

After completing medical school and becoming licensed to practice medicine (See *Physicians*), prospective gastroenterologists enter an internal medicine residency that lasts three years. Following residency, they must spend an additional two to three years in a gastroenterology fellowship. Competition for the available openings is fierce. According to Dr. Joseph Kirsner, a gastroenterologist with the University of Chicago Medical School, they receive 400 applications every year for the two or three openings.

Certification or Licensing

Certification, offered by the American Board of Internal Medicine (ABIM), is not required but is recommended, for it is a sign of professional excellence in the field. To become a board-certified gastroenterologist first requires certification in internal medicine. ABIM requirements for internal medicine certification are: graduation from an accredited medical school; three years of postdoctoral training; proven clinical competency; and passage of a comprehensive examination. Additional requirements for certification in the subspecialty of gastroenterology include three years of training in gastroenterology and passing a comprehensive subspecialty exam.

Other Requirements

Gastroenterologists must be able to communicate effectively with other health care professionals and with patients. This includes being a keen listener. A large part of successful treatment is accurate diagnosis, which requires carefully taken patient histories and close analysis of symptoms. Gastroenterologists must also be able to work with all types of people, and have a deep sense of caring and compassion.

Earnings

According to a 1998 survey conducted by the American Medical Association, the average net pay for internal medicine physicians is roughly $185,700, but salaries may begin around $116,306. Several factors influence earnings, including years of experience, geographic region of practice, and reputation. In general, those working in private practice earn more than those on staff at a hospital.

Outlook

Although the *Occupational Outlook Handbook* reports that physicians' careers are expected to grow faster than the average through the year 2006, the outlook for specialist physicians is not as bright. Managed care companies stress preventive medicine by primary care physicians over treatment by specialists, which can be very expensive. In response to this financial pressure, more medical students are choosing family practice residencies. Dr. Kirsner, for one, believes the effect of this shift will be temporary, and that patient demands for the best possible care will create openings for specialists in the more distant future.

Internal medicine is considered a primary care discipline and some gastroenterologists may be able to find work as internists. Dr. McNally and Dr. Kirsner both agree that there are fewer opportunities for gastroenterologists now than there were in the 1980s.

For More Information

For information on certification requirements, contact:

American Board of Internal Medicine
510 Walnut Street, Suite 1700
Philadelphia, PA 19106-3699
Tel: 800-441-2246
Web: http://www.abim.org

American Gastroenterological Association
7910 Woodmont Avenue, Suite 700
Bethesda, MD 20814
Tel: 301-654-2055
Web: http://www.gastro.org

American College of Gastroenterology
4900 B South 31st Street
Arlington, VA 22206
Tel: 703-820-7400
Web: http://www.acg.gi.org

General Practitioners

School Subjects
> Biology
> Health

Personal Skills
> Helping/teaching
> Technical/scientific

Work Environment
> Primarily indoors
> Primarily multiple locations

Minimum Education Level
> Medical degree

Salary Range
> $44,400 to $160,000 to $250,000

Certification or Licensing
> Required by all states

Outlook
> Faster than the average

Overview

General practitioners (GPs) are primary care physicians and may sometimes be referred to as *family practice physicians*. They are usually the first health care professional their patients consult for a problem. They treat people of all ages and tend to see the same patients on a continuing basis, often for years. General practitioners diagnose and treat any illness or injury that does not require the service of a specialist. They frequently serve as the family doctor, treating all the members of a family. In 1996, there were approximately 79,200 general practitioners.

History

While "family doctors" or the "general doc" have been a part of the health care picture ever since medicine began, today's efforts to control health care costs have led insurance companies to the increased use of Health Maintenance Organizations (HMOs) and Preferred Provider Organizations

(PPOs). These plans often limit the use of specialists, making subscribers seek care first from a primary care physician. Because of this, patients who might once have gone directly to a specialist without seeing a general practitioner must now see their general practitioner first in order to get a referral to see a specialist.

The Job

The general practitioner usually works with a staff of nurses and office personnel. Other physicians and medical personnel may be a part of the office setup as well. The GP sees patients ranging in age from newborns to the elderly. Unlike a specialist, the general practitioner treats the whole patient, not just a specific illness. The general practitioner may give the patient diet and lifestyle advice, as well as methods for preventing disease or injury. Some general practitioners may also provide prenatal care and deliver babies. The GP treats patients who have a wide variety of ailments and orders diagnostic tests and procedures, if necessary. If a patient comes in with an illness that requires special medical treatment, that patient is often referred to an appropriate specialist.

Usually about 70 percent of a general practitioner's work day is spent seeing patients in an office. They also treat patients in hospitals, confer with other medical personnel, patients, and family members, and perform limited surgery. Some practitioners might make house calls if the patient is unable to come to the office. In some private office situations, the general practitioner also oversees the office finances, equipment and supply purchases, and personnel. Many general practitioners must be on call to treat patients after regular office hours. If the GP works in a medical group they usually take turns being on call. General practitioners work long, irregular hours and can expect to put in 48 to 58 hours a week.

Requirements

Postsecondary Training

After receiving the M.D. degree (See *Physicians*), you must fulfill a one- to three-year hospital residency requirement where you are actively involved in patient treatment as part of a hospital medical team. At the end of an accredited residency program, physicians must pass certification examinations.

Certification or Licensing

In order to become licensed, a physician must graduate from an accredited medical school, complete at least one year of postgraduate training, and pass a licensing exam. Licensing examinations are given through the board of medical examiners in each state.

Other Requirements

To be a successful general practitioner, you should be committed to helping people, and be compassionate and understanding. You should have good communication skills to communicate with other staff members, patients, and their families, and be able to inspire their confidence and trust. In addition, a GP should have the stamina to work long and irregular hours.

Earnings

As a group, general practitioners' income usually is at the low end of the physician pay scale. According to the American Academy of Family Physicians, the average starting salary in 1997 was about $112,000 a year, and the average annual net income was $132,400 for established GPs. Recent surveys indicate that family physicians' salaries are rising.

Those affiliated with a group practice generally make more than those in solo practice and those who are self-employed may earn considerably more than salaried employees do. A general practitioner's income may be affected by years of experience and tends to peak between the ages of 46 and 55.

Physicians who are self-employed must provide their own insurance coverage. Those who are employed by an HMO, clinic, or other organization may receive a benefits package including insurance and paid time off.

Outlook

Employment of physicians is expected to grow faster than the average for all occupations through the year 2006. One reason for this growth is that the population is steadily increasing and people are living longer, requiring more health care services.

Job prospects are especially good for primary care physicians because more insurance companies are using HMOs and PPOs. These plans require that their insurance holders see a general practitioner first in order to get a referral to a specialist.

Because most physicians choose to practice in urban areas, these areas are often oversupplied and fiercely competitive. General practitioners just entering the field may find it difficult to enter a practice and build a patient base in a big city. There is a growing need, however, for physicians in rural communities and small towns, so general practitioners who are willing to locate in these areas should have excellent job prospects.

For More Information

The following organizations provide information on becoming a general practitioner.

American Academy of Family Physicians
8880 Ward Parkway
Kansas City, MO 64114
Tel: 816-333-9700
Web: http://www.aafp.org

American Medical Association
515 North State Street
Chicago, IL 60610
Tel: 312-464-5000
Web: http://www.ama-assn.org

American Osteopathic Association
142 East Ontario Street
Chicago, IL 60611
Tel: 312-280-5800
Web: http://www.aoa-net.org/

Association of American Medical Colleges
2450 N Street, NW
Washington, DC 10037
Tel: 202-828-0400
Web: http://www.aamc.org

Geriatricians

	School Subjects
Biology	
Health	
	Personal Skills
Helping/teaching	
Technical/scientific	
	Work Environment
Primarily indoors	
Primarily multiple locations	
	Minimum Education Level
Medical degree	
	Salary Range
$44,400 to $160,000 to $250,000	
	Certification or Licensing
Required by all states	
	Outlook
Faster than the average	

Overview

Geriatricians are physicians with specialized knowledge in the prevention, diagnosis, treatment, and rehabilitation of disorders common to old age. The term "geriatrics" refers to the clinical aspects of aging and the comprehensive health care of older people. It is an area of medicine that focuses on health and disease in old age and is a growing medical specialty. According to the American Geriatrics Association, there are currently 6,000 internists and 2,800 family physicians certified in geriatric medicine.

History

The term geriatrics comes from the Greek term, geras, meaning "old age," and iatrikos, meaning "physician." Formal training in geriatrics is relatively new. As our population ages, the need for physicians specializing in the care of older patients is growing. Today, life expectancy continues to advance and geriatricians are faced with medical and ethical challenges in the treatment of their patients.

The Job

Geriatricians spend most of their time with patients, taking patient histories, listening to their comments or symptoms, and running any of a number of diagnostic tests and evaluations, including physical examinations. Geriatricians generally see patients in a clinic, a long-term care facility, or a hospital. Each patient setting requires a unique type of patient care. Geriatricians often work with other physicians to diagnose and treat multiple problems and to provide the best possible care for each patient.

For example, an elderly man's complaint of fatigue could signal one or more of a large number of disorders. Diagnosis may be complicated by the coexistence of physical and mental problems, such as heart disease and dementia (mental confusion). This may mean consulting with a psychologist to treat the dementia and a cardiologist for the heart problems. Not only do geriatricians work with other medical personnel, they also work with family members and community services. Very often geriatricians work with the patient's family in order to get an accurate diagnosis, proper care, and follow-up treatment. If the patient is living alone, the geriatrician might also need the support of a social worker, neighbor, or relative to make certain that proper medication is administered and that the patient is monitored. If there is no cure for the patient's condition, the geriatrician must devise some way of helping the patient cope with the condition.

The job can be emotionally demanding and frustrating, as well as rewarding. Paperwork is also a large part of geriatricians' jobs as they must complete forms, sign releases, write prescriptions, and meet the requirements of Medicare and private insurance companies.

Requirements

Postsecondary Training

Geriatricians first earn an M.D. degree and become licensed to practice medicine (See *Physicians*). Then they must complete a residency in geriatrics, followed by formal training through one of over 150 geriatrics fellowship programs in the United States and Canada.

Certification or Licensing

A Certificate of Added Qualifications (CAQ) in Geriatric Medicine or Geriatric Psychiatry is offered through the certifying boards in family practice, internal medicine, osteopathic medicine, and psychiatry for physicians who have completed a fellowship program in geriatrics. The length of formal geriatrics training is linked to the individual's career goals in clinical care, teaching, or research, and can vary from 12 months to four years.

Other Requirements

The career of geriatrician is both intellectually and emotionally demanding. A good geriatrician needs to be able to effectively manage all aspects of a patient's problems, including social and emotional issues. Creative problem solving skills are an asset. Geriatricians must have a general interest in aging and the problems related to growing older. They should be effective communicators and listeners and be able to work as a team.

Earnings

Generally, the net median income for various physician specialties, according to 1995 American Medical Association figures, ranges between $124,000 to $230,000. There are no available income figures specific to geriatricians. There is a large demand for geriatricians, and due to this high demand, physicians specializing in gerontology may earn more than these averages.

Outlook

Job opportunities for individuals who enter geriatrics will likely grow at a rate much faster than the average. The U.S. Bureau of the Census estimates that the number of individuals age 65 or older will double by the year 2050. Therefore, the need for the expert care given by geriatricians is expected to grow. Physicians will be spending a greater percentage of time treating older patients as this elderly population increases. In addition, older people tend to require more medical services than younger people do, so the geriatrician career field is full of promise.

For More Information

The following organizations provide information on geriatrician careers.

Alzheimer's Association
919 North Michigan Avenue, Suite 1000
Chicago, IL 60611
Tel: 312-335-8700
Web: http://www.alz.org

American Association for Geriatric Psychiatry
7910 Woodmont Avenue, Suite 1050
Bethesda, MD 20814
Tel: 301-654-7850
Web: http://www.aagpgpa.org

American Federation for Aging Research
1414 Avenue of the Americas, 18th Floor
New York, NY 10019
Tel: 212-752-2327
Web: http://www.afar.org

American Geriatrics Society
770 Lexington Avenue, Suite 300
New York, NY 10021
Tel: 212-308-1414
Web: http://www.americangeriatrics.org

Hematologists

—School Subjects

Biology
Chemistry

—Personal Skills

Helping/teaching
Technical/scientific

—Work Environment

Primarily one location
Primarily indoors

—Minimum Education Level

Medical or doctoral degree

—Salary Range

$124,000 to $180,000 to
$230,000

—Certification or Licensing

Required by all states (for MDs)

—Outlook

Little change or more slowly than
the average

Overview

Hematologists study and/or treat diseases of the blood and the blood-forming tissues. Some hematologists are physicians (M.D.s) who specialize in blood diseases; other hematologists are medical scientists (Ph.D.s) who do research on blood diseases but do not treat patients. A few students who plan to focus on medical research choose to do a joint M.D./Ph.D. program.

History

Hematology is classified as a subspecialty of internal medicine (the branch of medicine that studies and treats, usually by nonsurgical means, diseases of the body's internal organs). This exciting, high-tech field in medical research has made dramatic advances in recent decades. Many forms of leukemia that would formerly have meant death within a few months of diagnosis are now curable because of research performed by hematologists.

The Job

Some hematologists are medical scientists who do blood-related research but do not treat patients. Others are physicians who have chosen to specialize in blood diseases and their treatment. Some physicians in hematology concentrate on work with patients, while others are more research oriented and work primarily in research laboratories.

The duties of a hematologist depend on whether you are a research scientist or a medical doctor. In the case of a doctor, it also depends on whether you are primarily involved in research or in patient treatment. As a subspecialty of internal medicine (the branch of medicine that studies and treats diseases of the body's internal organs), hematology is also closely connected with oncology, the internal medicine subspecialty dealing with tumors. Hematology and oncology are often combined into a single department in medical schools. Some doctors specialize in pediatric hematology-oncology, working exclusively with children who have blood disorders and/or cancer.

If you work in an academic research setting, your principal responsibility might be conducting research, which also includes supervising the lab and the people who work in it, writing grants to get federal money to fund the lab, as well as other responsibilities, such as giving lectures and teaching.

Requirements

High School

Future scientists and physicians should take college prep courses in high school. Laboratory sciences (biology, chemistry, physics) and mathematics are especially important as the foundation for more advanced work later. English, foreign languages, history, and other humanities and social sciences courses are important as well. Good oral and written communication skills are also essential.

Postsecondary Training

A premed program is best if you plan to go to medical school. If there is no premed program, or if you want to pursue a Ph.D. program, then chemistry or biology is an appropriate undergraduate major. Some colleges also offer undergraduate majors in biochemistry, microbiology, or genetics.

You must take the Medical College Admission Test (MCAT) before applying to medical school and the Graduate Record Exam (GRE) before applying to graduate school. Apply to at least three medical or graduate schools to increase your chances of acceptance.

Medical school and Ph.D. programs in the biomedical sciences generally take at least four years. A combined M.D./Ph.D. program usually takes six to seven years.

After graduating from medical school, students spend at least two years in a hospital residency program. The length of the residency period depends on the specialty chosen. Because hematology is a subspecialty of internal medicine, a three-year residency in general internal medicine followed by two years of training in a hematology or hematology-oncology program is required.

Certification or Licensing

After graduating from medical school, you need to pass the licensing examination administered through the board of medical examiners in the state where you plan to practice. If you want to be certified in a medical specialty, you need to pass the specialty board examination in your field after completing residency requirements.

For medical scientists who are not M.D.s, the Ph.D. is generally considered your "license."

Other Requirements

The hematologist should have an inquiring mind and an interest in medicine and research as well as strong academic ability, especially in the sciences. You should have the discipline to spend long hours writing lengthy grant proposals and researching articles. You should also have the ability to be a team player and have patience to conduct lengthy research projects. If you are working directly with patients and their families, you should feel comfortable dealing with seriously ill people.

Employers

Hematologists are employed at medical centers, university medical schools, private research institutes, and blood banks. Hematologists who are physicians have a wider range of employment opportunities than scientists since they also have the option of clinical practice in addition to, or instead of, research.

Starting Out

Hematologists find out about job openings in their field through personal contacts and professional journals. Sometimes a postdoctoral fellowship turns into a permanent job. The competition for research positions at prestigious institutions is keen; there can be hundreds of applicants for one job.

The ability to attract grant money for one's lab and all or part of one's salary plays a major role in a hematologist's employability. Occasionally, it is even necessary to raise one's own funding for a postdoctoral position.

Advancement

Hematologists advance by developing and carrying out research that is recognized as significant by their professional peers and that has the ability to draw grant money from the federal government and private foundations. Some hematologists move into administrative positions and become directors of major research projects.

Those in academic positions advance by moving from assistant professor to associate professor to full professor. In this field, the most important criteria for academic promotion would be research achievements. Hematologists (or hematologist-oncologists) who are involved in clinical work advance in their profession as more patients are referred to them for specialized treatment.

Earnings

There are no specific salary figures for hematologists; however, physicians are among the highest paid professionals. Generally, the median net income for various specialties according to 1995 American Medical Association figures ranges from $124,000 to $230,000. Physicians in clinical work tend to earn much more than hematologists who concentrate on research do. The pay for research scientists is sometimes based on available grant or research funds.

Benefits may be available through the research institute, medical practice, or professional association.

Work Environment

Hematologists often work in research laboratories as independent researchers and as part of a team. These laboratories can be part of a university, hospital, or government research facility. They may also be part of a teaching staff at a university or medical college. Hematologists who are physicians work in clinics, as part of a group practice, or as a member of a hospital or research team.

Outlook

The job outlook for hematologists is difficult to predict. There are many blood disease questions still to be solved, but the future of research depends on the availability of funding.

Another factor that makes the future of this field unpredictable is the fact that other subspecialties are taking over some of the areas previously handled by hematologists. For instance, the relationship between hematology and oncology is growing closer, which could result in hematology eventually being absorbed into oncology. Another example is that coagulation (blood clotting) problems are being taken over by cardiology and neurology because of the role of clotting in heart disease and strokes.

It should be noted, however, that physicians continue to have one of the lowest unemployment rates of any profession.

For More Information

The following organizations provide information on the field of hematology.

American Society of Hematology (ASH)
1200 19th Street, NW, Suite 300
Washington, DC 20036
Tel: 202-857-1118
Web: http://www.hematology.org

American Board of Internal Medicine
510 Walnut Street, Suite 1700
Philadelphia, PA 19104
Tel: 215-446-3500
Web: http://www.abim.org

Holistic Physicians

The Job

Holistic physicians are licensed medical doctors who embrace the philosophy of treating the patient as a whole person. Their goal is to help the individual achieve maximum well-being for the mind, body, and spirit. Holistic medicine emphasizes a cooperative relationship between physician and patient and focuses on educating patients in taking responsibility for their lives and their health. Holistic physicians use many approaches to diagnosis and treatment, including alternative approaches such as acupuncture, meditation, nutritional counseling, and lifestyle changes.

In many ways, the primary duties of holistic physicians are much like those of allopathic physicians (conventional doctors). They care for the sick and injured and counsel patients on preventive health care. They take medical histories, examine patients, and diagnose illnesses. Holistic physicians also prescribe and perform diagnostic tests and prescribe medications. They refer patients to specialists and other health care providers as needed. They use conventional drugs and surgery when less invasive approaches are not appropriate or effective.

An important difference between the practices of allopathic physicians and holistic physicians is the approach to the patient/doctor relationship. Holistic doctors work in partnership with their patients, usually spending more time with their clients than allopathic doctors do. Holistic doctors usually spend 45 minutes to an hour or more on an initial visit, while follow-up visits average 30 to 45 minutes.

During the initial history and physical, holistic physicians ask questions about all aspects of a person's life. They want to know about eating and sleeping habits, lifestyle, stress, emotions, beliefs, goals, and much more. They also ask about your family's health history as well as your own. Holistic physicians don't just want to know today's symptoms; they want to find the underlying causes of those symptoms. They listen very carefully, and they do not make personal judgments about their patients' lives.

Holistic doctors use healing modalities that consider the whole person and support the body's natural healing capabilities. They use a variety of approaches to diagnosis and treatment. For chronic (long-term) problems, they frequently recommend natural methods of treatment that have been shown to be more effective than conventional approaches. They are usually trained in several alternative health modalities themselves, but they may refer patients to a specialist if their expertise is not adequate.

Requirements

Postsecondary Training

Holistic physicians must meet the same educational requirements as convential physicians. At the present time, training for competency in holistic or alternative medicine is not a part of regular medical training, but nearly one-third of all conventional medical schools now include some courses in alternative therapies. Most holistic physicians train themselves in alternative modalities through special postgraduate work and continuing education. A few graduate schools now offer specialized programs in alternative health care approaches.

Certification

At this time, there is no special certification or licensing available for holistic physicians. A practitioner's decision to use the term "holistic physician" or "alternative physician" is strictly voluntary. The American Holistic Medical Association (AHMA) established the American Board of Holistic Medicine

(ABHM) in 1996. The ABHM has developed a core curriculum on which it will base board certification for holistic physicians, beginning in the near future.

Earnings

Holistic physicians generally earn about as much as allopathic physicians who work in the same settings. Some holistic practitioners may earn less because they spend more time with their patients, so they can see fewer in a day. Some make up the difference by charging more per visit. Others may earn less because they work fewer hours or days—in keeping with their belief in the importance of a balanced lifestyle. Holistic physicians tend to work 40 to 50 hours a week, while their conventional counterparts work 50 to 60 hours or more.

Outlook

According to the 1998-99 *Occupational Outlook Handbook* (OOH), employment for physicians will grow faster than the average for all occupations through the year 2006. Demand for holistic physicians can be expected to keep pace with or exceed the demand for conventional physicians due to the recent rapid growth in interest in alternative health care approaches.

For More Information

For articles on holistic health, self-help resources in the United States, and a searchable database of practitioner members, contact:

American Holistic Health Association (AHHA)
Department R, PO Box 17400
Anaheim, CA 92817-7400
Tel: 714-779-6152
Web: http://ahha.org

For principals of holistic medical practice, the proposed board certification for holistic medicine, and a searchable database of members, contact:

American Holistic Medical Association (AHMA)
6728 Old McLean Village Drive
McLean, VA 22101
Tel: 703-556-9728
Web: http://www.holisticmedicine.org

Neurologists

School Subjects	Biology Health
Personal Skills	Helping/teaching Technical/scientific
Work Environment	Primarily indoors Primarily multiple locations
Minimum Education Level	Medical degree
Salary Range	$44,400 to $160,000 to $250,000
Certification or Licensing	Required by all states
Outlook	Faster than the average

Overview

Neurologists are physician specialists who diagnose and treat patients with diseases and disorders affecting such areas as the brain, spinal cord, peripheral nerves, muscles, and autonomic nervous system.

History

The development of modern neurology began in the 18th and 19th centuries. Studies were performed on animals in order to understand how the human brain functioned. Although these early studies produced some useful information, major research in the field of neurology did not begin until the end of the 19th century. Aphasia, epilepsy, and motor problems were targeted and researched. Techniques for brain mapping were also introduced in an effort to determine the locations of functional areas.

In the early 1920s, Hans Berger invented the electroencephalograph, which records the electrical activity in the brain. This achievement led to greater capabilities in diagnosis, treatment, and rehabilitation. During the late 20th century, neurology was further advanced by computerized axial tomography (CAT scans), nuclear magnetic resonance (NMR), and neurosurgery. Continued research has led to better drug therapies and a clearer understanding of brain function.

The Job

A neurologist evaluates, diagnoses, and treats patients with diseases and disorders impairing the function of the brain, spinal cord, peripheral nerves, muscles, and autonomic nervous system, as well as the supporting structures and vascular supply to these areas. A neurologist conducts and evaluates specific tests relating to the analysis of the central or peripheral nervous system.

In addition to treating such neurological disorders as epilepsy, neuritis, brain and spinal cord tumors, multiple sclerosis, Parkinson's disease, and stroke, neurologists treat muscle disorders and pain, especially headache. Illnesses, injuries, or diseases that can adversely affect the nervous system, such as diabetes, hypertension, and cancers, are also treated by neurologists.

Neurologists see patients in two capacities—as a consulting physician or as the patient's principal physician. A neurologist works as a consulting physician when asked by a patient's primary care physician to consult on a case as, for example, when a patient has a stroke or shows signs of mental confusion. As a consulting physician, the neurologist conducts a neurological examination and evaluates mental, emotional, and behavioral problems to assess whether these conditions are treatable. The neurologist also works with psychiatrists, psychologists, or other mental health professionals as necessary.

Requirements

Postsecondary Training

Neurologists first earn an M.D. degree and become licensed to practice medicine (See *Physicians*). Those physicians who choose to specialize in neurology must first complete a full year of training in internal medicine in a program approved by the Accreditation Council for Graduate Medical Education (ACGME). Then, the physician must enroll in an accredited, three-year neurology residency program. As an alternative to this prescribed training, the physician may complete four years of training in an ACGME-approved neurology program. These residency programs provide supervised neurology experience in both hospital and ambulatory (outpatient) settings. Educational conferences and research training are also part of a neurology residency.

Certification or Licensing

Upon completion of residency training, neurologists may seek certification from the American Board of Psychiatry and Neurology (ABPN). To be eligible for certification, qualified applicants must have an unrestricted state license to practice medicine, the required years of residency training; and must pass both a written and oral examination as administered by the ABPN.

Other Requirements

Because they treat patients who have suffered injuries to the head, neurologists need to have a calm and soothing presence with patients who may be experiencing alternating emotions, including confusion and anger. In addition to compassion, neurologists need to be capable of sifting through a lot of data for specific details.

Earnings

According to a 1998 survey conducted by the American Medical Association, the average net income for neurologists is about $175,000, but salaries may range from $152,000 to $190,200. These figures are only a guide. Individual salaries will vary depending on such factors as type and size of practice, geographic area, and professional reputation.

Work Environment

Neurologists, like many physicians, must divide their time between patient consultations, study and publishing, and office or departmental administration. Most neurologists work far more than 40 hours a week. A neurologist may see anywhere between 10 and 30 patients each day. They perform medical histories, diagnose problems, and explain treatment and rehabilitation options.

Outlook

The health care industry is thriving and according to the *Occupational Outlook Handbook,* the employment of physicians is expected to grow faster than the average for all occupations through 2006. In particular, the specialty of neurology should increase. In the United States, neurologic illnesses make up 15 to 20 percent of all general medical care. As effective therapies are developed for more neurological diseases, and some diseases, such as Alzheimer's, increase in prevalence, the demand for neurologists will increase.

For More Information

Following are organizations that provide information on the certification and profession of neurologist:

American Academy of Neurology
1080 Montreal Avenue
St. Paul, MN 55116
Tel: 612-695-1940
Web: http://www.aan.com

The American Board of Psychiatry and Neurology, Inc.
500 Lake Cook Road, Suite 335
Deerfield, IL 60015
Tel: 847-945-7900
Web: http://www.abpn.com

Obstetricians and Gynecologists

School Subjects
| Biology
| Health

Personal Skills
| Helping/teaching
| Technical/scientific

Work Environment
| Primarily indoors
| Primarily multiple locations

Minimum Education Level
| Medical degree

Salary Range
| $44,400 to $160,000 to $250,000

Certification or Licensing
| Required by all states

Outlook
| Faster than the average

Overview

A physician who specializes in obstetrics and gynecology is trained to deliver babies and provide medical and surgical care for disorders that affect the female reproductive system, the fetus, or the newborn.

History

Obstetrics and gynecology were recognized medical disciplines in the United States by the middle of the 19th century. However, these two fields developed separately throughout history and differently across cultural boundaries.

Female midwives were the first individuals to perform obstetric work. It was not until the 17th century that European physicians became involved in childbirth. Aristocrats and royalty allowed these physicians to attend the births of their children and eventually the practice spread to the middle classes.

Gynecology evolved separately from obstetrics, but was practiced in Greco-Roman civilization and possibly earlier. Despite their separate early histories, the similar nature of obstetrics and gynecology forced the disciplines to merge. Both fields were advanced by the invention of the forceps used during delivery, anesthesia, and antiseptic methods used during gynecologic surgery and childbirth. Asepsis's method of cesarean section as an alternative to natural childbirth was also a major advancement in early medical practice.

Fertility, the promotion of healthy births, and prenatal care define the scope of obstetric and gynecologic advances during the 20th century. Hormonal contraceptive pills were introduced in the 1950s and helped to regulate women's fertility, while the development of amniocentesis and ultrasound allowed for more accurate prenatal diagnosis of birth defects.

The Job

The specialty of obstetrics and gynecology can be divided into two parts. Obstetrics focuses on the care and treatment of women before their pregnancy, during the pregnancy, and after the child is born. Gynecology is concerned with the treatment of diseases and disorders of the female reproductive system. Because the areas overlap, the specialties are generally practiced together. Preventive measures and testing make up a large part of an obstetrician/gynecologist's practice.

Obstetrician/gynecologists provide many different types of health services to women, from prenatal care to Pap tests to screening tests for sexually transmitted diseases (STDs) to breast exams and birth control. With specialization, the obstetrician/gynecologist's practice may focus on pregnant patients, cancer patients, or infertile patients.

Disorders that obstetrician/gynecologists commonly treat include yeast infections, pelvic pain, endometriosis, infertility, and uterine and ovarian cancer. An obstetrician/gynecologist prescribes medicines and other therapies and if necessary, schedules and performs surgery.

When an examination and test indicates that a patient is pregnant, an obstetrician/gynecologist sets up regular appointments with the patient throughout the pregnancy. These visits make up a crucial part of any woman's prenatal care, helping her learn about her pregnancy, nutrition and diet, and activities that could adversely affect the pregnancy. In addition, the patient is examined to see that the pregnancy is progressing normally. Later in the pregnancy, the frequency of visits increases, and they become important in determining a birthing strategy and any alternate plans. An obstetrician/gynecologist will deliver the baby and care for the mother and child after the delivery.

Requirements

Postsecondary Training

To become an obstetrician/gynecologist you must first earn an M.D. degree and become licensed to practice medicine (See *Physicians*). Then you must complete a minimum of four years in residency, three of them entirely in obstetrics and gynecology, with a one-year elective.

After completing a residency in obstetrics and gynecology, a specialist in obstetrics and gynecology may pursue additional training to subspecialize in critical care medicine, gynecologic oncology, maternal-fetal medicine, or reproductive endocrinology.

Certification and Licensing

Certification by the American Board of Obstetrics and Gynecology (ABOG) is highly recommended. In the last months of your residency, you take the written examination given by the ABOG. Candidates for certification take the final oral examination after two or more years of practice. You must have successfully passed the written portion of the certifying exam before you are eligible to take the oral portion.

Other Requirements

Communication skills are essential as most of your time is spent with patients, talking to them and listening to their histories and problems. The intimate nature of both the patient's condition and the examination requires that an obstetrician/gynecologist be able to put the patient at ease while asking questions of an intimate nature.

Earnings

Salaries for obstetrician/gynecologists vary according to the kind of practice (whether the obstetrician/gynecologist works individually or as part of a group practice), the amount of overhead required to maintain the practice, and the geographic location. According to a 1998 survey conducted by the American Medical Association, the average net pay for an obstetrician/gynecologist is about $231,000, but salaries may range from $145,000 to $238,312.

Outlook

The general population is aging, and health care needs increase dramatically with age. The health care industry, in general, is doing exceptionally well, despite the claims of managed care critics to the contrary. According to the *Occupational Outlook Handbook,* the employment of all physicians in almost all fields is expected to grow faster than the average for all occupations through 2006. Salaries, however, are predicted to drop somewhat due to managed care.

Specifically, the demand for obstetrician/gynecologists has not abated. The specialty is shifting from a male-dominated field to a female-dominated field; of the medical students planning to enter obstetrics and gynecology, 60 percent are now women.

For More Information

These organizations provide information on the obstetrics/gynecology profession.

American Board of Obstetrics and Gynecology (ABOG)
2915 Vine Street
Dallas, TX 75205
Tel: 214-871-1619
Web: http://www.abog.org

American College of Obstetricians and Gynecologists (ACOG)
409 12th Street, SW
Washington, DC 20024
Tel: 202-638-5577
Web: http://www.acog.org

Oncologists

School Subjects
Biology
Health

Personal Skills
Helping/teaching
Technical/scientific

Work Environment
Primarily indoors
Primarily multiple locations

Minimum Education Level
Medical degree

Salary Range
$44,400 to $160,000 to $250,000

Certification or Licensing
Required by all states

Outlook
Faster than the average

Overview

Oncologists are physicians who study, diagnose, and treat the tumors caused by cancer.

History

The history of cancer dates back to early Greek and Roman writings, which included descriptions of the disease. It is clear that cancer affects all of the world's populations and has been the subject of intense medical investigations. At least one million new cases of invasive cancer are diagnosed each year and cancer ranks only second to heart disease as the leading cause of death.

Developments in the late 20th century, such as improvements in cancer treatment and early detection, have advanced the discipline of oncology and led to further studies. In the 1950s, minor success with cytotoxic chemotherapy initiated active research to develop anticancer agents. Although most useful drugs have side effects, oncologists continue to conduct studies to find better treatments and many believe that cancer is a largely preventable disease.

The Job

An oncologist is a physician, such as a doctor of internal medicine, who specializes in the study, diagnosis, and treatment of cancerous tumors. Because cancer can affect any organ in the body, and individuals of any age, there are many different kinds of oncologists. For example, *medical oncologists* have studied internal medicine and treat cancer through chemotherapy. *Pediatric oncologists* are pediatricians who specialize in cancers that affect infants and children. *Gynecological oncologists* are gynecologists who specialize in cancers that attack the female reproductive organs, including the ovary, cervix, and uterus. *Radiological oncologists* treat tumors through radiation therapy. *Surgical oncologists* are surgeons who specialize in removing cancerous tissue to prevent its growth. There are many other subspecialties within the practice of oncology. In fact, there are almost as many different subspecialties of oncology as there are different kinds of doctors.

A *clinical oncologist* conducts clinical trials in order to identify the most successful strategies for fighting cancer. Clinical trials are studies that are conducted on consenting patients. By comparing the results of two different treatments on two groups of patients with similar symptoms, clinical oncologists are able to determine which methods are more effective in eliminating or retarding the development of cancer.

Because cancer can spread throughout the organs of the body, oncologists often work together in teams to identify the appropriate strategy for helping a patient. Many patients undergo a combination of chemotherapy, radiation therapy, and surgery to treat cancer, so it is extremely important for the physicians to coordinate the treatment process.

Requirements

Postsecondary Training

Oncologists must first earn an M.D. degree and become licensed to practice medicine (See *Physicians*). Following an internship year, doctors complete a residency in a specialty. For example, someone interested in gynecologic oncology completes a four-year obstetrics and gynecology residency. Someone interested in medical oncology, on the other hand, does a residency in internal medicine. Following the residency, the doctor completes a fellowship (specialized study) in oncology. A fellowship in gynecologic oncology, for example, can take from two to four years to complete.

Certification or Licensing

Certification is not required for oncologists, but it is highly recommended. Certification for oncologists is administered by boards in their area of specialty. For example, certification for medical oncologists is administered by the American Board of Internal Medicine. Certification for gynecologic oncologists is administered by the American Board of Obstetrics and Gynecology, Inc.

Other Requirements

Oncologists must be extremely hard working, perceptive, and emotionally balanced individuals. They must also be voracious readers with excellent memories, as new information about the cause, prevention, and treatment of cancer is published each day. Staying current with new information also requires that the oncologist be proficient with technology, easily able to access new information through the medium of the computer. An oncologist's own researching and writing skills must be well developed, because publishing research results is an important way to advance in this profession.

In addition to the intellectual rigors of the job, oncologists must be prepared to accept emotional and psychological challenges. Each day, they interact with people who are very ill and frightened. They must be able to maintain objectivity and composure under intensely emotional circumstances. Because oncologists must explain very complex information to people who have little or no scientific background, they also must be able to communicate clearly and directly. Excellent interpersonal skills will help the oncologist work as part of a medical team. A surgical oncologist, for example, may have to work with a medical team that includes a dietician, a physical therapist, the original referring doctor, nurses, and other staff members.

Earnings

According to a 1998 survey conducted by the American Medical Association, the average net pay for an oncologist is about $196,749, but salaries may range from $176,200 to $260,860. Individual earnings of oncologists will vary, depending on such factors as geographic location, years of experience, professional reputation, and type of oncology practiced.

Fringe benefits for oncologists typically include health and dental insurance, paid vacations, and retirement plans.

Outlook

Due to a growing and aging population, new research, changing diagnostic techniques, and new treatment possibilities, oncology is a rapidly growing field. According to the *Occupational Outlook Handbook,* positions in oncology are abundant and are projected to grow at a faster than average rate in the 21st century.

For More Information

Following are organizations that provide information on the profession of oncology.

American Society of Clinical Oncology
225 Reinekers Lane, Suite 650
Alexandria, VA 22314
Tel: 703-299-0150
Web: http://www.asco.org

Radiation Therapy Oncology Group
American College of Radiology
1101 Market Street, 14th Floor
Philadelphia, PA 19107
Tel: 215-574-3150
Web: http://www.rtog.org

Ophthalmologists

Biology Health	School Subjects
Helping/teaching Technical/scientific	Personal Skills
Primarily indoors Primarily multiple locations	Work Environment
Medical degree	Minimum Education Level
$44,400 to $160,000 to $250,000	Salary Range
Required by all states	Certification or Licensing
Faster than the average	Outlook

Overview

Ophthalmologists are physicians who specialize in the care of eyes and in the prevention and treatment of eye disease and injury. They test patients' vision and prescribe glasses or contact lenses. Most ophthalmologists perform eye surgery to remove cataracts, which cloud vision, or to correct other problems. Ophthalmologists often work with other physicians because in examining the eyes, they may discover signs of diseases affecting other parts of the body.

History

Ophthalmology is an ancient medical specialty that dates back to around 1600 BC, when many vision problems were already recognized. The treatments that were available at the time were primitive, such as using crocodile dung and lizard blood to treat eye problems. Since then, treatments have gradually advanced.

Although the surgeon Susruta performed cataract surgery in India more than 2,000 years ago, Western Europe did not develop the specialty until the mid-1800s. During this era, a solid base of scientific research and medical advances in ophthalmology evolved. The ophthalmoscope, which is an instrument used to view the inside of the eye, was developed during this time.

Ophthalmology has undergone numerous significant scientific and technological breakthroughs during the past 10 years or so. Retinal laser surgery is one recent groundbreaking procedure that has become a common practice among ophthalmologists.

The Job

Most ophthalmologists spend four days a week in the office seeing patients and one day a week performing surgery, usually at a hospital. Office visits typically involve performing eye examinations and screening for diseases and infections such as glaucoma and conjunctivitis, or pink eye. Part of the job of ophthalmologists is to prevent vision problems, so many of their patients may not wear glasses but come in for an annual exam.

Most ophthalmologists treat patients of all ages, from infants to elderly adults. During an examination, they will check a patient's vision and will prescribe glasses and contact lenses to correct any problems. They will also screen for diseases using tools such as an ophthalmoscope, which is an instrument used to look at the inside of the eye. When examining a patient's eyes, the ophthalmologist could discover signs of disease that affect other parts of the body including diabetes and hypertension. When that happens, the ophthalmologist may work with another physician in diagnosing and managing the disease.

In a typical workweek, an ophthalmologist will see over 100 patients and perform two major surgeries. The most common surgery that ophthalmologists perform is to remove cataracts, which are a clouding of the lens of the eye that causes partial or total blindness. Cataract surgery lasts just 30 minutes to an hour and usually helps patients regain all or some of their vision. Ophthalmologists also perform surgery to correct crossed eyes and glaucoma.

The practice of ophthalmology also involves treating patients who have diseases that could cause them to lose some or all of their vision. That possibility can make patients feel fearful and anxious and can create stress for both the patients and the doctor. Ophthalmologists should be able to show patients compassion and understanding in offering their medical expertise.

Requirements

Postsecondary Training

There is often confusion over the difference between an ophthalmologist and an optometrist. Ophthalmologists have medical degrees, while optometrists do not. After earning an M.D. degree and becoming licensed to practice medicine (See *Physicians*), ophthalmologists complete at least one year of general clinical training, and at least three years in an eye residency program at a hospital. Often ophthalmologists work at least one more year in a subspecialty fellowship.

Certification or Licensing

Certification by the American Board of Ophthalmology is not required, but it is highly recommended. Most hospitals will not let ophthalmologists practice if they are not certified. To receive the board's certification, a candidate needs to complete the ophthalmology residency and written and oral examinations given by the board. Ophthalmologists must reapply for certification every 10 years.

Other Requirements

Certain visual and motor skills are necessary to be an ophthalmologist. Without good motor skills, depth perception and color vision, an ophthalmologist may have trouble using instruments that are part of the practice. If you like to do needlework or build models, you may have the skills needed to perform surgery. Ophthalmologists need to be patient and good at communicating with people, too.

Earnings

Ophthalmologists' salaries vary by the kind of hospital where they work and by the city or town where they practice. Other factors affecting salary include the type and size of the ophthalmologist's practice, hours worked per week, and professional reputation. Salaries for ophthalmologists range from

$31,000 (for residents) to $140,000 and can reach $200,000 and up. The national average salary for surgeons in the mid-1990s ranged from approximately $140,000 to $300,000.

Outlook

In 1998, there were approximately 18,000 ophthalmologists in the United States, according to the American Academy of Ophthalmology. A little over 2 percent of M.D.s specialize in ophthalmology.

The employment outlook for all doctors is projected to be "faster than average" growth through 2006, according to the 1998-99 *Occupational Outlook Handbook*. The increasing number of elderly people will drive the demand for physicians. New technology will allow doctors to conduct more tests and treat more conditions that were previously untreatable.

The demand for ophthalmologists, as for other specialists, depends on advances in medicine and how much health insurance and vision care plans provide for primary eye care.

For More Information

For information on careers and certification, contact the following:

American Academy of Ophthalmology
655 Beech Street
San Francisco, CA 94109
Tel: 415-561-8500
Web: http://www.eyenet.org

American Board of Ophthalmology
111 Presidential Boulevard, Suite 241
Bala Cynwyd, PA 19004
Tel: 610-664-1175

American Society of Contemporary Medicine, Surgery and Ophthalmology
4711 West Golf Road, Suite 408
Skokie, IL 60076
Tel: 847-568-1500
Web: http://www.ascmso.com

Optometrists

Biology Physics	School Subjects
Helping/teaching Technical/scientific	Personal Skills
Primarily indoors Primarily one location	Work Environment
Doctor of Optometry degree	Minimum Education Level
$57,500 to $65,000 to $92,600+	Salary Range
Required by all states	Certification or Licensing
Faster than the average	Outlook

Overview

An *optometrist* is a health care professional who provides primary eye care services. These services include comprehensive eye health and vision examinations; diagnosis and treatment of eye diseases and vision disorders; the prescribing of glasses, contact lenses, low-vision rehabilitation, vision therapy, and medications; the performing of certain surgical procedures; and the counseling of patients regarding their vision needs. By examining the eyes, optometrists may also identify signs of diseases and conditions that affect the entire body.

History

Modern optometry is derived from the work of a number of Europeans in the 19th century who were interested in measuring the eye and in inventing instruments for testing sight. Research in physics, mathematics, and optics helped early optometrists make significant discoveries. As they became better known in the field, professional organizations were formed to gain legal recognition for optometry and to establish education programs for optometrists.

Two particular landmarks in the development of the profession of optometry are noteworthy. A national association of optometrists was first formed in 1897. In 1901, Minnesota passed the first state law regulating the practice of optometry. Today, every state as well as the District of Columbia has such a law.

The number of optometrists has continued to grow to meet the demands of the increasing population in the United States.

The Job

Optometrists are primarily concerned with examining eyes and performing other services to safeguard and improve vision. To do this, they use special tests and instruments to identify and evaluate eye health, including visual acuity, depth and color perception, and ability to focus and coordinate the eyes. They prescribe what should be done to correct vision problems, which may include prescriptions for eyeglasses, contact lenses, vision therapy, or therapeutic drugs. They diagnose eye diseases caused by systemic conditions such as diabetes or high blood pressure. Optometrists refer these patients to other specialists.

Optometrists are one of three professional groups involved in treatment of the eyes. *Ophthalmologists* are medical school graduates with specialized training in working with the medical and surgical care of the eyes. They prescribe drugs, perform surgery, diagnose and treat eye diseases, and prescribe lenses and exercises.

Opticians use the prescriptions provided by ophthalmologists and optometrists to grind lenses, assemble the eyeglasses, and fit and adjust them.

Some optometry specialties include work with the elderly, children, or partially sighted persons who need specialized visual devices to improve their vision, treatment of workplace injuries, contact lenses, sports vision, or vision therapy. A few teach optometry, do research, or consult.

Most optometrists are in general practice. Those who have private practices must also handle the business aspects of running an office, such as developing a patient base, hiring employees, keeping records, and ordering equipment and supplies. Optometrists who operate franchise optical stores may also have some of these duties.

Requirements

Postsecondary Training

Three years of college plus four years in a school or college of optometry is the minimum requirement for becoming an optometrist. The first three years of college are generally devoted to course work in mathematics, physics, biology, and chemistry, as well as the other general education subjects studied by students in colleges of liberal arts and sciences. The professional degree program is devoted to laboratory, classroom, and clinical work in the field of optometry. Upon completion of study, graduates receive the doctor of optometry (O.D.) degree. Some optometrists pursue further study leading to a master's degree or doctorate in physiological optics or other fields.

Certification or Licensing

Before individuals can practice as optometrists, they must secure a license in the state in which they wish to practice. To do this, they must pass an examination prepared by the state. Individuals cannot take the examination unless they are graduates of a school or college of optometry recognized by the state in question. All states and the District of Columbia require an individual to have a state license to practice optometry.

To be eligible to take the licensing examination, an individual must be a graduate of an accredited school or college of optometry. The licensing examination is administered by a state board of optometry and generally covers the following subjects: ocular anatomy, ocular pathology (disease), optometric methods, theoretical optometry, psychological optics, physical and geometrical optics, physiological optics, physiology, and optometrical mechanics. It also includes a clinical examination. In all states as well as the District of Columbia, optometrists must earn continuing education credits in optometry to renew their licenses. Optometry is the only health care profession that has the universal continuing education requirement for license renewal. The most frequently recognized exam is given by the National Board of Examiners in Optometry.

Other Requirements

Prospective optometrists must be able to get along well with people. Their practices will often depend on how people regard them. The optometrist must also have mechanical aptitude and good vision and coordination. These characteristics are essential to the training required to become licensed.

Exploring

It is difficult for students to gain any direct experience on a part-time basis in optometry. The first opportunities afforded students generally come in the clinical phases of their training program. Interested students, however, can explore the desirability of a career in optometry in several ways. They can visit an optometrist's office and talk to an experienced optometrist. Part-time or summer work in an optical store or in an optometrist's practice will also expose students to the work environment and routines, as well as give them greater opportunities of talking with optometrists and technicians.

Employers

Currently, there are approximately 34,000 licensed optometrists in the United States. The vast majority are employed in private practice, but others work in health clinics, industries, the armed forces, and schools and colleges of optometry.

Starting Out

There are several ways of entering the field of optometry once an individual has a license to practice. Most optometrists set up their own practices or purchase an established practice. Other beginners serve as associates to established optometrists until they gain enough experience and financial resources to establish their own practices. Some work in health maintenance organizations (HMOs). Still other beginners work in government-supported clinics or in the armed forces. Some students of optometry earn their doctorates and go directly into research and teaching in schools and colleges of optometry.

Advancement

Optometrists may advance in their profession by specializing in one area. Or they may move from being an associate optometrist to establishing their own practice.

Optometrists in good standing are eligible for membership in the American Optometric Association, which is the major professional organization for optometrists. A smaller number of optometrists who meet very rigid requirements are also eligible for membership in the American Academy of Optometry. Optometrists also hold membership in state and local optometric societies.

Earnings

Currently, the earnings of new optometry graduates average about $57,500 a year. The average earnings for experienced optometrists is about $92,600. Optometrists in group practice or partnerships often earn substantially higher incomes than optometrists practicing alone.

Graduates of schools and colleges of optometry who accept salaried positions with clinics and government agencies generally have higher earnings in the first few years than do private practitioners. This situation, however, often changes after the private practitioners have had an opportunity to establish themselves.

Work Environment

Optometrists generally have excellent working conditions, and their work is not strenuous. They often work in their own offices and are free to set their own office hours and to arrange their vacations and free time. The optometrist usually works in quiet surroundings and is seldom faced with emergencies. Although most optometrists still have solo practices, some have chosen to work in partnerships or teams to alleviate the rising cost of set-up, insurance, and repayment of school loans.

Outlook

The employment outlook for optometrists is expected to be favorable through 2006. The demand for eye care services will become greater as people continue to become more health conscious. Also, people are more likely to seek such services because they are better able to pay for them as a result of higher income levels, the growing availability of employee vision-care plans, and Medicare law allowing coverage for optometrists' services. Increased use of computers by people of all ages appears to lead to eyestrain and aggravated vision problems, creating more need for optometrists. A growing elderly population, the group most likely to need eyeglasses, also will keep demand strong. Some of the needed eye care will be provided by physicians who specialize in the treatment of the eyes, but there will be more than ample opportunity for optometrists to supply a substantial amount of service.

For More Information

For information on optometry careers and educational programs, contact:

American Optometric Student Association
243 North Lindbergh Boulevard
St. Louis, MO 63141-7881
Tel: 314-991-4100
Web: http://www.aoanet.org/aoanet

Association of Schools and Colleges of Optometry
6110 Executive Boulevard, Suite 510
Rockville, MD 20852
Tel: 301-231-5944
Web: http://www.opted.org

For information on the entrance exam and the Optometric Admissions Test (OAT), contact:

Optometry Admission Testing Program
211 East Chicago Avenue, Suite 1846
Chicago, IL 60611-2678
Tel: 312-440-2693

Canadian Association of Optometrists
11830 Kingsway Avenue, Suite 902
Edmonton, Alberta G5G 0X5 Canada
Tel: 403-451-6824

Osteopaths

Biology
Psychology
————————————————School Subjects

Helping/teaching
Technical/scientific
————————————————Personal Skills

Primarily indoors
Primarily one location
————————————————Work Environment

Medical degree
————————————————Minimum Education Level

$35,000 to $166,000 to
$250,000+
————————————————Salary Range

Required by all states
————————————————Certification or Licensing

Much faster than the average
————————————————Outlook

Overview

Osteopaths practice a medical discipline that uses refined and sophisticated manipulative therapy based on the late 19th century teachings of American Dr. Andrew Taylor Still. It embraces the idea of "whole person" medicine and looks upon the system of muscles, bones, and joints—particularly the spine—as reflecting the body's diseases and as being partially responsible for initiating disease processes. Osteopaths are medical doctors with additional specialized training in this unique approach. They practice in a wide range of fields, from environmental medicine, geriatrics, and nutrition to sports medicine and neurology, among others.

History

Osteopathy has its roots in the hardships and challenges of 19th-century America. Its developer, Dr. Andrew Taylor Still, was born in 1828 in Virginia. There were few medical schools in the United States, so Still received his early medical training largely from his father. As the Civil War began, he attended the College of Physicians and Surgeons in Kansas City, but he enlisted in the army before completing the course.

In 1864, an epidemic of meningitis struck the Missouri frontier. Thousands died, including Still's three children. His inability to help them underscored his growing dissatisfaction with traditional medical approaches. After much careful study of anatomy, physiology, and the general nature of health, he became convinced that cultivating a deep understanding of the structure—function relationship between the parts of the body was the only path to a true understanding of disease. Eventually, Still came to believe in three basic principles that would form the core of his osteopathic approach to the practice of medicine. First, he saw the body as capable of self-healing, producing its own healing substances. Second, he felt health was dependent upon the structural integrity of the body. And, finally, because of these beliefs, he considered distorted structure a fundamental cause of disease.

A system of physical manipulation was an integral component of Still's new practice. He began to compare manipulative therapy with other methods then used by doctors, such as drugs and surgery. Often, he found the use of manipulative methods made drugs and operations unnecessary. Instead, he focused on the musculoskeletal system—the muscles, bones, nerves, and ligaments. Recognizing that structural misalignments often occurred in these areas, he emphasized the system's importance as a major potential factor in disease, ripe for the application of his new manipulative techniques.

Still founded the first college of osteopathy in Kirksville, Missouri, in 1892, basing it upon the fundamental principles of his osteopathic concept. Fewer than 20 men and women graduated from this first osteopathic college in 1894. Today, there are 19 osteopathic schools in the United States. Some are part of major university campuses, and combined, they accept roughly 2,500 new osteopathic students annually.

Although practitioners of alternative methods of healing in the United States were—and sometimes still are—seen as a threat by the medical profession, osteopathy has increased in popularity. As the field grew, some students wished to use drugs as well as osteopathic techniques in treating patients. John Martin Littlejohn, for example—a Scotsman who studied with Still—widened the focus of osteopathy by concentrating not only on anatomy, but stressing physiological aspects as well. Unlike Still, Littlejohn wanted osteopaths to learn all about modern medicine, along with osteopathic principles and practices. Later, Littlejohn returned to Britain, where he founded the British School of Osteopathy. Even so, the training of osteopaths in the United States was, in fact, eventually to merge with the training of orthodox medical physicians.

The Job

Osteopathy and orthodox medicine both use the scientific knowledge of anatomy and physiology, as well as clinical methods of investigation. In this respect, they have a similar language. The greatest differences, however, lie in the way patients are evaluated and in the approach to treatment. As a general rule, the orthodox medical approach focuses on the end result of the problem: the illness. Treatments seek to repair the imbalance presented by the illness through the prescription of drugs or by surgery. In contrast, osteopaths focus on tracing the changes in a patient's ability to function that have occurred over a period of time. This is done to understand the chain of events that have altered the relationship between structure and function, resulting in the patient's present complaint. The primary aim of treatment is to remove the obstacles within a patient's body that are preventing the natural self-healing process from occurring. It's a subtle difference, but important.

Like most physicians, as an osteopath, you'll probably spend much of your day seeing patients in a clinic or hospital setting. Your specialty, of course, may take you to other venues—nursing homes or sports arenas, for instance.

Your first task in evaluating a new patient is trying to understand the cause of the problem that the patient presents. To arrive at an appropriate diagnosis, the history you take as an osteopath will likely be greatly detailed—remember, the osteopath needs to consider the whole body. It is precisely that concern for seemingly irrelevant details, coupled with manipulative therapy, which distinguishes the osteopath (or D.O.) from the allopath (or conventional M.D.)

One technique that assists in the correct evaluation of patient problems is palpation, a manual means of diagnosis and determination, whereby sensory information is received through the fingers and hands. Along with careful listening and observation, palpation will help you assess healthy tissue and identify structural problems or painful areas in your patient's body.

The osteopath differs from a traditional M.D. or allopathic physician in one other major aspect—treatment options. For the D.O., treatment centers around what are called osteopathic lesions. Osteopathic lesions are functional disturbances in the body, involving muscles, joints, and other body systems. They are not lesions as M.D.s refer to them—incursions, cuts, or other tissue damage—but are created by mechanical and physiological reactions in the body to various types of trauma. In osteopathy, open, unhindered, and balanced movement is the most important factor in health. The lack of it plays a major role in the onset of disease and illness. Thus, the many varied techniques employed by osteopaths are concerned primarily with re-establishing normal mobility and removing or reducing the underlying lesions.

Requirements

High School

Students who plan a career as a physician—either as a D.O. or an M.D.—should take a college preparatory program in high school. You'll need a strong foundation in the sciences, especially biology, chemistry, and physics. In addition, take English, history, foreign languages, and all the math you can. Psychology is a helpful course in preparing you to work well with a wide variety of people coming to you for treatment.

Postsecondary Training

For persons with bachelor's degrees, the American Association of Colleges of Osteopathic Medicine offers prospective medical students a centralized application service for the 19 accredited osteopathic medical schools. Students file one application along with a single set of transcripts and MCAT (Medical College Admission Test) scores. The service will verify and distribute your application to those colleges you designate. You should be aware that admission to an osteopathic medical school, like all medical schools, is quite competitive. Over 9,500 applicants submitted a total of more than 55,000 applications in 1997. Only a combined total of 2,500 seats were available to first-year students.

Once you're in, the academic program leading to the Doctor of Osteopathy degree involves four years of study, followed by a one-year rotating internship in areas such as internal medicine, obstetrics/gynecology, and surgery. If you're interested in a specific specialty, an additional two to six years of residency training is required.

The curriculum in colleges of osteopathic medicine supports Dr. Still's osteopathic philosophy, with an emphasis on preventive, family, and community medicine. Clinical instruction stresses examining all patient characteristics (including behavioral and environmental), and how various body systems interrelate. Close attention is given to the ways in which the musculoskeletal and nervous systems influence the functioning of the entire body. An increasing emphasis on biomedical research in several of the colleges has expanded opportunities for students wishing to pursue research careers.

Certification or Licensing

At an early point in the residency period, all physicians, both M.D.s and D.O.s, must pass a state medical board examination in order to obtain a license and enter practice. Each state sets its own requirements and issues its own licenses, although some states will accept licenses from other states.

Many osteopathic physicians belong to the American Osteopathic Association (AOA). To retain membership, physicians must complete 150 hours of continuing education every three years. Continuing education can be acquired in a variety of ways, including attending professional conferences, completing education programs sponsored by the AOA, osteopathic medical teaching, and publishing articles in professional journals.

The AOA offers board certification. Certification has many requirements, including passing a comprehensive written exam as a well as a practical test in which you must demonstrate osteopathic manipulative techniques. The AOA offers specialty certification in more than 100 specialty areas. Some osteopathic physicians are certified by both the AOA and the American Medical Association (AMA).

Other Requirements

There are a few other things to keep in mind if you're considering a career in osteopathy. For instance, the practice of osteopathy usually involves a lot of personal interaction, and a lot of touching, which can make some patients—and some prospective doctors—feel uncomfortable. Osteopathic physicians need excellent communication skills to tell patients what to expect and what is happening at any one moment. Good communication skills are also necessary to do the best job informing your patients about the right kind of treatment. If patients don't understand what you're telling them, they may not pursue the treatment. You need to learn to work well with others and to be a perceptive listener.

Since a large number of osteopaths go into private practice, business and management skills are useful. In addition, good manual dexterity is important to use manipulative techniques for the patient's optimum benefit. Finally, and most importantly, you must have a real commitment to caring for people in this way. A lesser goal may not be enough to help see you through the sometimes difficult and always long days of training.

Exploring

Consider visiting an osteopathic medical college. Tours are often available and can give you extra insight into necessary training and the ways in which life at an osteopathic medical school differs from a "regular" one. If you don't live close enough to an osteopathic college to visit, write for more information.

Check into after-school or summer jobs at your local hospital or medical center. Any job that exposes you to the care of patients is a good one, even jobs you might not think of at first, or ones that aren't exactly medical, such as working with the janitorial service. Contact the American Osteopathic Association and ask for a list of osteopaths in your area. Talk to as many people as you can and don't be afraid to ask questions.

Employers

Osteopaths can be found in virtually all medical specialties. They use the most modern scientific methods to understand and treat their patients' problems, and this means they often are hired by a wide variety of institutions. Many—more than one-third—go into private practice after completing their training. They also work in hospitals, clinics, nursing homes, and other health care settings. Anywhere you can find an M.D., you probably also can find a D.O.

Starting Out

For a newly graduated physician, the first step beyond medical school and internship is additional schooling. Depending upon the specialty in which you're interested, you can plan on completing a residency program of two to six years' duration. Gaining admission to the program you want may be a challenge. One of the difficulties facing the profession today is that its schools produce more students than there are available spaces for residents at osteopathic hospitals. Graduates of osteopathic hospitals must increasingly find residencies in traditional medical facilities—where some osteopaths feel that it's more difficult to adhere to the unique philosophy that is central to their training. As awareness of and interest in osteopathy continue to grow, this situation may change. After residency, you can choose to go into private practice or explore positions with a variety of health care employers.

Advancement

Advancement in the medical professions is dependent on the specific field you're in. Osteopaths in private practice will follow a different career path than those working in a purely clinical setting, who live still a different life than osteopaths who choose a research-oriented career at an academic medical center. As noted earlier, a large percentage of osteopaths go into private or small-group practice. Advancement in private practice is largely what you make of it. As your practice grows, you'll earn the satisfaction of knowing patients in your community are well cared for. You'll set your career goals yourself. In contrast, osteopaths in employee positions are more limited by the type of job they've taken.

Earnings

Osteopaths earn incomes comparable to their M.D. counterparts, and the potentially high income of an established physician can be an enticing perk of becoming an osteopath. Median net income (after expenses but before taxes) in 1996 was $166,000 for all M.D.s in clinical practice. Some make less, many make more. There are a number of other factors you might want to keep in mind, however, as described in a recent survey of the American Medical Association. Counting postgraduate education, most physicians are in their early thirties before starting to practice. Residency pay is low, yet residents worked an average of 80 to 100 hours per week. Most physicians incur high educational debt by the time they begin to practice. Eighty-two percent of 1996 graduates reported some level of debt, with the average amounting to $75,103.

Benefits for osteopathic physicians vary, depending on whether they work in private practice or for an employer. In general, it depends, too, on how you define benefits. The AMA survey indicates that median net income for self-employed physicians is approximately 40 percent higher than that of employee physicians.

Work Environment

As with the benefits you earn, the environment in which you work can vary as an osteopath. During your training, you will be highly supervised; eventually you will be deemed to have garnered the knowledge necessary to work on your own. In both private practice and employer-based situations, you will sometimes work alone (e.g., directly with your patient) and sometimes be part of a team. Osteopathy, like all medical professions, is a field of contrasts, requiring both collaboration and personal insight. If you enjoy the idea of becoming a physician, a wide array of work environments will be open to you as an osteopath. What's the primary obstacle to be aware of going in? It's no surprise: some extraordinarily long hours, particularly during training.

Outlook

The records of the American Association of Colleges of Osteopathic Medicine show the number of osteopathic graduates has increased 50 percent in the last decade, making osteopathic medicine one of the fastest-growing health professions in the country. To meet the growing demand, more than a dozen new osteopathic medical colleges have opened their doors since the mid-1970s. Together, all 19 institutions currently enroll more than 8,000 students annually, of whom nearly 35 percent are women.

Although osteopathic medicine is not strictly an "alternative" approach, the field is benefiting from the current interest in these kinds of therapy. Excellent job opportunities will continue to become available for skilled osteopathic physicians. In addition to specialized practices in areas such as family medicine, increasing interest in biomedical research at the osteopathic colleges also is expanding opportunities for candidates interested in careers in medical research.

For More Information

This association publishes a college information booklet and a financial aid guide. A good deal of general information is accessible through the association's Web site.

American Association of Colleges of Osteopathic Medicine
5550 Friendship Boulevard, Suite 310
Chevy Chase, MD 20815
Tel: 301-968-4100
Web: http:\\www.aacom.org

The AOA Web site offers many short booklets on family health topics as well as osteopathic medicine.

American Osteopathic Association
Department of Communications
142 East Ontario Street
Chicago, IL 60611
Tel: 312-202-8000 or 800-621-1773
Web: http:\\www.am-osteo-assn.org

Pathologists

School Subjects
| Biology
| Health

Personal Skills
| Helping/teaching
| Technical/scientific

Work Environment
| Primarily indoors
| Primarily multiple locations

Minimum Education Level
| Medical degree

Salary Range
| $44,400 to $160,000 to $250,000

Certification or Licensing
| Required by all states

Outlook
| Faster than the average

Overview

Pathologists are physicians who analyze tissue specimens to identify abnormalities and diagnose diseases.

History

During the late Middle Ages, the earliest known autopsies were performed to determine cause of death in humans. As these autopsies were documented, much information about human anatomy was gathered and studied. In 1761, the culmination of autopsy material resulted in the first textbook of anatomy by Giovanni Batista Morgagni.

Many developments in pathology occurred during the 19th century, including the discovery of the relationship between clinical symptoms and pathological changes. In 1958, Ruldolf Virchow revealed the significance of the microscopic analysis of cells. Louis Pasteur and Robert Koch later developed the bacteriologic theory, which was fundamental to understanding disease processes. By the late 19th century, pathology was a recognized medical specialty.

Technological advances of the 20th century, from electron microscopes to computers, have led to further growth and developments in the field of pathology.

The Job

Pathologists provide information that helps physicians care for patients; because of this, the pathologist is sometimes called the "doctor's doctor." When a patient has a tumor, an infection, or symptoms of a disease, a pathologist examines tissues from the patient to determine the nature of the patient's condition. Without this knowledge, a physician would not be able to make an accurate diagnosis and design the appropriate treatment. Because many health conditions first manifest themselves at the cellular level, pathologists are often able to identify conditions before they turn into serious health problems.

Many people associate pathologists only with the performing of autopsies. In fact, while pathologists do perform autopsies, much of their work involves living patients. Pathologists working in hospital laboratories examine the blood, urine, bone marrow, stools, tissues, and tumors of patients. Using a variety of techniques, pathologists locate the causes of infections and determine the nature of unusual growths. Pathologists consult with a patient's physician to determine the best course of treatment. They may also talk with the patient about his or her condition. In a sense, the work of pathologists is much like detective work. It is often through the efforts of pathologists that health conditions are recognized and properly treated.

Requirements

Postsecondary Training

Like any medical specialist, a pathologist must earn an M.D. degree and become licensed to practice medicine (See *Physicians*), after which begins a four-year pathology residency. Residents may choose to specialize in anatomical pathology or clinical pathology. Many pathologists, however, prefer to specialize in both anatomical and clinical pathology; licensing as an AP/CP pathologist requires a five-year residency. Various subspecialties require further training beyond the residency.

Certification and Licensing

A pathologist can pursue certification along three primary paths—an anatomic pathology program, a clinical pathology program, or a combined anatomic and clinical pathology program. Once a pathologist has completed certification, he or she can choose to specialize in a particular area of pathology. Gaining certification in a specialty generally requires an additional one to two years of training, although there is a potential for combining this training with the standard pathology residency program.

Other Requirements

Successful pathologists should have an eye for detail and be able to concentrate intently on work, work well and communicate effectively with others, and be able to accept a great deal of responsibility. They need to perform well under pressure, be patient, thorough, and confident in decisions.

Earnings

According to a 1998 survey conducted by the American Medical Association, the average net pay for a pathologist is about $212,200, but salaries may range from $169,138 to $232,432. Several factors influence earnings, including years of experience, geographic region of practice, and reputation.

Outlook

According to the *Occupational Outlook Handbook*, physicians' careers are expected to grow faster than the average through 2006. The outlook for careers in pathology is particularly good. New medical tests are constantly being developed and refined, making it possible to detect an increasing number of diseases in their early stages. The medical community depends on pathologists to analyze results from these tests. Another factor favorably affecting the demand for pathologists is the shifting of health care to cost-conscious managed care services. Testing for, diagnosing, and treating a disease or other health condition in its early stages is much less expensive than treating a health condition in its advanced stages.

For More Information

Following are organizations that provide information on pathology careers, accredited schools, and employers:

American Board of Pathology
PO Box 25915
Tampa, FL 33622
Tel: 813-286-2444
Web: http://www.abpath.org

College of American Pathologists
325 Waukegan Road
Northfield, IL 60093
Tel: 847-832-7000
Web: http://www.cap.org

Intersociety Committee on Pathology Information
4733 Bethesda Avenue, Suite 730
Bethesda, MD 20814
Tel: 301-656-2944
Web: http://www.pathologytraining.org

United States and Canadian Academy of Pathology
3643 Walton Way Extension
Augusta, GA 30909
Tel: 706-733-7550
Web: http://www.uscap.org

Pediatricians

Biology Health	School Subjects
Helping/teaching Technical/scientific	Personal Skills
Primarily indoors Primarily multiple locations	Work Environment
Medical degree	Minimum Education Level
$44,400 to $160,000 to $250,000	Salary Range
Required by all states	Certification or Licensing
Faster than the average	Outlook

Overview

Pediatricians are physicians who provide health care to infants, children, and adolescents. Typically, a pediatrician meets a new patient soon after birth, and takes care of that patient through his or her teenage years.

History

Children became the focus of separate medical care during the 18th century in Europe. Children's health care became a recognized medical specialty during the early 19th century, and by the middle of the 19th century, pediatrics was taught separately in medical schools. The first pediatric clinic in the United States opened in New York City in 1862. About that same time, several children's hospitals opened in Europe.

Studies focused on developing treatments for infectious diseases of childhood such as measles and scarlet fever. By the beginning of the 20th century, pediatricians began promoting the normal growth and development of children. Well-child clinics began to open around the United States.

Some of the most significant breakthroughs in children's health care have been in disease prevention. By the middle of the 20th century, the development of vaccines and antibiotics greatly decreased the threat of infectious diseases.

The Job

A significant part of a pediatrician's job is preventive medicine—what is sometimes called "well care." This involves periodically seeing a patient for routine health checkups. During these checkups, the doctor physically examines the child to make sure he or she is growing at a normal rate and to look for symptoms of illness. The physical examination includes testing reflexes, listening to the heart and lungs, checking eyes and ears, and measuring height and weight.

During the checkup, the pediatrician also assesses the child's mental and behavioral development. This is done both by observing the patient's behavior and by asking the parents questions about their child's abilities.

Immunizing children against certain childhood diseases is another important part of preventive medicine. Pediatricians administer routine immunizations for such diseases as rubella, polio, and smallpox, as children reach certain ages. Yet another part of preventive medicine is family education. Pediatricians counsel and advise parents on the care and treatment of their children. They provide information on such parental concerns as safety, diet, and hygiene.

In addition to practicing preventive medicine, pediatricians also treat sick infants and children. When a sick or injured patient is brought into the office, the doctor examines him or her, makes a diagnosis, and orders treatment. Common ailments include ear infections, allergies, feeding difficulties, viral illnesses, respiratory illnesses, and gastrointestinal upsets. For these and other illnesses, pediatricians prescribe and administer treatments and medications.

If a patient is seriously ill or hurt, a pediatrician arranges for hospital admission and follows up on the patient's progress during the hospitalization. In some cases, a child may have a serious condition, such as cancer, cystic fibrosis, or hemophilia, that requires the attention of a specialist. In these cases, the pediatrician, as the primary care physician, will refer the child to the appropriate specialist.

Some pediatric patients may be suffering from emotional or behavioral disorders or from substance abuse. Other patients may be affected by problems within their families, such as unemployment, alcoholism, or physical abuse. In these cases, pediatricians may make referrals to such health professionals as psychiatrists, psychologists, and social workers.

Some pediatricians choose to pursue pediatric subspecialties, such as the treatment of children who have heart disorders, kidney disorders, or cancer. Subspecialization requires a longer residency training than does general practice. A pediatrician practicing a subspecialty typically spends a much greater proportion of his or her time in a hospital or medical center than does a general practice pediatrician. Subspecialization permits pediatricians to be involved in research activities.

Requirements

Postsecondary Training

After earning an M.D. degree and becoming licensed to practice medicine (See *Physicians*), pediatricians must complete a three-year residency program in a hospital. The pediatric residency provides extensive experience in ambulatory pediatrics, the care of infants and children who are not bedridden. Residents also spend time working in various specialized pediatric units, including neonatology, adolescent medicine, child development, psychology, special care, intensive care, and outpatients.

Some of the other subspecialties a pediatrician might acquire training for include adolescent medicine, pediatric cardiology (care of children with heart disease), pediatric critical care (care of children requiring advanced life support), pediatric endocrinology (care of children with diabetes and other glandular disorders), pediatric neurology (care of children with nervous system disorders), pediatric hematology/oncology (care of children with blood disorders and cancer), and neonatology.

Certification or Licensing

Certification by the American Board of Pediatrics (ABP) is recommended. A certificate in General Pediatrics is awarded after three years of residency training and the successful completion of a two-day comprehensive written examination. A pediatrician who specializes in cardiology, infectious diseases, or other areas must complete an additional three-year residency in the subspecialty before taking the certification examination. To remain board-certified, pediatricians must pass an examination every seven years.

Other Requirements

To be a successful pediatrician, you should like children and adolescents; have patience, compassion, and a good sense of humor; be willing to continually learn; have a desire to help others; and be able to withstand stress and make sound decisions.

Earnings

Pediatricians, while at the low end of the earning scale for physicians, still have among the highest earnings of any occupation in the United States.

According to a 1998 survey conducted by the American Medical Association, the average net pay for pediatricians is about $140,600, but salaries may range from $105,375 to $142,595. The earnings of pediatricians are partly dependent upon the types of practices they choose. Those who are self-employed tend to earn more than those who are salaried. Geographic region, hours worked, number of years in practice, professional reputation, and personality are other factors which can impact a pediatrician's income.

Outlook

According to the *Occupational Outlook Handbook,* physician's jobs are expected to grow faster than the average through the year 2006. The employment prospects for pediatricians—along with other general practitioners, such as family physicians—are especially good. This is because of the increasing use of managed care plans which stress preventive care.

For More Information

Following are organizations that provide information on pediatric careers, accredited schools, and employers:

American Academy of Pediatrics
141 Northwest Point Boulevard
Elk Grove Village, IL 60007
Tel: 847-228-5005
Web: http://www.aap.org

American Pediatric Society
3400 Research Forest Drive, Suite B7
The Woodlands, TX 77381
Tel: 281-296-0244
Web: http://www.aps-spr.org

Ambulatory Pediatric Association
6728 Old McLean Village Drive
McLean, VA 22101
Tel: 703-556-9222
Web: http://www.ambpeds.org

Periodontists

School Subjects
| Chemistry
| Health

Personal Skills
| Helping/teaching
| Technical/scientific

Work Environment
| Primarily indoors
| Primarily one location

Minimum Education Level
| Medical degree

Salary Range
| $119,000 to $130,000 to
| $145,000

Certification or Licensing
| Required by all states

Outlook
| About as fast as the average

Overview

Periodontists are dentists who specialize in the diagnosis and treatment of diseases affecting the gums and bone that support the teeth. They perform thorough clinical examinations, measuring the depth of gum pockets and checking for gingival bleeding, and may do tests to find out which types of bacteria are involved. Periodontal surgery may be needed in more severe cases of periodontitis. Some periodontists also insert dental implants to replace lost teeth.

History

Although the field of periodontology was formalized in the early 20th century, periodontal disease and treatment have been recognized throughout history. For thousands of years, it was thought that build-ups of calculus, or tartar, were responsible for periodontal disease. Many old civilizations documented periodontal diseases or treatment methods.

In the late 1800s, periodontal surgery techniques were developed and diagnosis was improved by the use of X rays. In recent years, digital radiography and superimposed X-ray images have enhanced the effectiveness of X rays. Surgical methods have also been refined, and lasers are now used in place of scalpels in certain procedures. About 20 to 25 years ago, a multitude of diagnostic procedures were established. Periodontal researchers have developed methods to regenerate lost bone in recent years.

In recent years it has been confirmed that bacterial infection, not calculus build-up, causes periodontal disease. Periodontists now use antibiotics, either in pill form or placed inside the periodontal pocket.

When treatment fails and a tooth must be extracted, dental implants offer a new way of replacing the tooth; artificial teeth or dentures may be attached to implants.

An intensive area of periodontal research today is the relationship between gum disease and medical conditions, including heart disease and premature births. Chronic exposure to periodontal bacteria and inflammation may make people more susceptible to other diseases.

Future research may provide a vaccine to prevent periodontal infections.

The Job

Periodontists perform thorough clinical examinations, using calibrated periodontal probes to measure periodontal pocket depths and the "attachment level" of periodontal tissues. They check for gingival bleeding, evaluate the amount of plaque and calculus, and assess tooth stability. They also take X rays to see if the patient has bone loss from past periodontal disease. Periodontists may do tests to find out which types of bacteria are involved.

Meticulous removal of calculus below the gum line, or scaling, remains an important part of treatment. Root planing is a more intensive form of scaling that involves removing infected cementum from root surfaces. When their periodontal disease has been stabilized, patients enter the maintenance phase of treatment and return every few months for scaling and root planing.

Periodontists also prescribe antibiotics to eliminate bacteria in the periodontal pockets. Increasingly, antibiotics are placed directly in the pocket in the form of fibers, gels, or chips.

Periodontal surgery may be needed in more severe cases of periodontitis. Periodontics has been one of the most surgically oriented dental specialties, but this may change as more effective antibiotic treatments become available.

Periodontists also can surgically insert bone-regenerating materials into areas with bone loss to grow new bone. This process is known as guided tissue regeneration.

When periodontal disease is left untreated or treatment fails, tooth loss may occur. Periodontists and other dentists can replace lost teeth with dental implants, which are metal or ceramic-metal devices surgically inserted into the jawbone. Artificial teeth or dentures are attached to the implants to restore normal function.

Periodontists may also perform cosmetic procedures, such as reshaping the gum line to make the teeth appear longer in patients with "gummy" smiles.

Those who manage their own practices must hire, train, and supervise employees, including office staff and dental hygienists.

Requirements

Postsecondary Training

To enter dental school, applicants generally need significant college course work in the sciences, a bachelor's degree, and a good score on the Dental Admissions Test, or DAT. After completing four years of dental school, dentists who want to specialize in periodontics attend a three-year graduate training program.

Certification or Licensing

Before entering practice, dentists must pass a licensing examination. Qualified candidates may also seek certification by the American Board of Periodontology.

Other Requirements

Periodontists, like other dentists, must have excellent hand-eye coordination and the ability to do finely detailed work. As procedures and technology change, practicing periodontists must continue life-long learning. They stay up to date on advances in their specialty by taking continuing education courses each year. Also, because many dentists own their own practices, knowledge of business practices is beneficial.

Employers

Like general dentists, more than 90 percent of periodontists are in private practice. They may have a solo practice or work in a group practice with other dentists. Dentists serving in the military treat members of the military and their families. The U.S. Public Health Service also employs dentists to provide care or conduct research. Periodontists may also teach full-time or part-time in dental schools. Hospitals employ dentists to treat hospitalized patients. Periodontists may work in scientific research or administration at universities, private or government research institutes, and dental product manufacturers.

Starting Out

After completing dental school and an advanced training program in periodontology, most periodontists either start their own practices or join an established practice. While many dentists choose to have their own practices, start-up costs can be steep: new dentists often need to borrow money to buy or lease office space and buy expensive equipment.

Advancement

Periodontists in private practice advance their careers by building their reputation among the general dentists who refer patients to specialists. To establish a good reputation, it is important to communicate effectively and coordinate treatment with general dentists.

Periodontists who teach at dental schools may advance in academic rank and eventually chair the department of periodontology.

Experienced periodontists and periodontal researchers can become more prominent through professional activities such as writing scientific books and articles and being active in professional organizations such as the American Academy of Periodontology.

Earnings

According to the American Dental Association Survey Center, periodontists under age 40 have an average net salary of about $119,000. This represents the lower end of the salary range. Periodontists who have been in practice for some time generally have higher earnings; the average net salary for periodontists over age 40 is $145,000.

Salaries also vary by geographic region and are influenced by the number of other periodontists practicing in a community.

Benefits vary by place of employment. Self-employed periodontists often arrange their own benefits through their dental practices.

Work Environment

Most periodontists work in private dental practices. The hours worked vary; some practitioners work only part-time, perhaps because they also teach part-time or are nearing retirement. Others work full-time and may treat some patients in the evening or on weekends.

While many dentists wear comfortable business attire underneath a laboratory coat, some opt to wear surgical scrubs when treating patients.

Periodontists may travel from time to time to attend continuing education courses or meetings held by professional organizations.

Outlook

The demand for periodontists is expected to remain relatively steady, but the procedures that they perform may change over time. As Americans retain more teeth and live longer, they have more teeth at risk for periodontal disease. Furthermore, as the possible links between chronic periodontal infection and medical diseases become more widely known, people may be more motivated to receive regular periodontal care.

Periodontal surgery is expected to be less common as more patients are managed with antibiotics and preventive care. This is good news for patients because periodontal surgery is expensive, but may mean reduced income for periodontists.

Lasers allow periodontists to perform some surgical procedures with less bleeding, pain, and scarring. Periodontists who use lasers in their practices may attract patients who prefer laser surgery to conventional procedures.

Some periodontists treat tooth loss with dental implants. Many patients are willing to pay out-of-pocket for implants because they want an alternative to wearing a conventional denture or bridge.

For More Information

This professional organization for specialists in periodontics sponsors the Journal of Periodontology, *scientific workshops, continuing education programs, and annual meetings.*

American Academy of Periodontology
737 North Michigan Avenue
Chicago, IL 60611
Tel: 312-787-5518
Web: http://www.perio.org

This primary professional organization for dentists promotes dental health and the dental profession through education, research, and advocacy. It publishes the Journal of the American Dental Association *and* ADA News.

American Dental Association
Department of Career Guidance
211 East Chicago Avenue
Chicago, IL 60611
Tel: 312-440-2500
Web: http://www.ada.org/tc-educ.html

Physician Assistants

	School Subjects
Biology Health	

	Personal Skills
Helping/teaching Technical/scientific	

	Work Environment
Primarily indoors Primarily multiple locations	

	Minimum Education Level
Some postsecondary training	

	Salary Range
$30,000 to $62,000 to $100,000	

	Certification or Licensing
Required by all states	

	Outlook
Faster than the average	

Overview

Physician assistants practice medicine under the supervision of licensed doctors of medicine or osteopathy, providing various health care services to patients. Much of the work they do was formerly limited to physicians.

History

Physician assistants are fairly recent additions to the health care profession. The occupation originated in the 1960s when many medical corpsmen received additional education enabling them to help physicians with various medical tasks. Since then, the work of the physician assistant has grown and expanded; in addition, the number of physician assistants in the United States has greatly increased. Fewer than 100 PAs were practicing in 1970; today there are more than 24,000.

The Job

Physician assistants, also known as PAs, help physicians provide medical care to patients. PAs may be assigned a variety of tasks; they may take medical histories of patients, do complete routine physical examinations, order laboratory tests, draw blood samples, give injections, decide on diagnoses, choose treatments, and assist in surgery. Although the duties of PAs vary by state, they always work under the supervision and direction of a licensed physician. The extent of the PA's duties depends on the specific laws of the state and the practices of the supervising physician, as well as the experience and abilities of the PA. PAs work in a variety of health care settings, including hospitals, clinics, physicians' offices, and federal, state, and local agencies.

About 50 percent of all PAs specialize in primary care medicine, such as family medicine, internal medicine, pediatrics, obstetrics and gynecology, and emergency medicine. Nineteen percent of all PAs work in surgery or surgical subspecialties. In 1998, 41 states and the District of Columbia allowed PAs to prescribe medicine to patients. In California, prescriptions written by PAs are referred to as written prescription transmittal orders. Physician assistants may be known by other occupational titles such as child health associates, MEDEX, physician associates, anesthesiologist's assistants, or surgeon's assistants.

PAs are skilled professionals who assume a great deal of responsibility in their work. By handling various medical tasks for their physician employers, PAs allow physicians more time to diagnose and treat more severely ill patients.

Requirements

Postsecondary Training

Most states require that PAs complete an educational program approved by the Commission on Accreditation of Allied Health Education Programs (CAAHEP). In 1998, there were 104 fully accredited PA programs, and 24 programs with provisional accreditation. Admissions requirements vary, but two years of college courses in science or health, and some health care experience, are usually the minimum requirements. More than half of all students accepted, however, have their bachelor's or master's degrees. Most educational programs last 24 to 25 months, although some last only one year and others may last as many as three years.

The first six to 24 months of most programs involve classroom instruction in human anatomy, physiology, microbiology, clinical pharmacology, applied psychology, clinical medicine, and medical ethics. In the last nine to 15 months of most programs, students engage in supervised clinical work, usually including assignments, or rotations, in various branches of medicine, such as family practice, pediatrics, and emergency medicine.

Graduates of these programs may receive a certificate, an associate's degree, a bachelor's degree, or a master's degree; most programs, however, offer graduates a bachelor's degree. The one MEDEX program that presently exists lasts only 18 months. It is designed for medical corpsmen, registered nurses, and others who have had extensive patient-care experience. MEDEX students usually obtain most of their clinical experience by working with a physician who will hire them after graduation.

PA programs are offered in a variety of educational and health care settings, including colleges and universities, medical schools and centers, hospitals, and the armed forces. State laws and regulations dictate the scope of the PA's duties, and, in all but a few states, PAs must be graduates of an approved training program.

Certification or Licensing

Currently, all states—except Mississippi—require that PAs be certified by the National Commission on Certification of Physician Assistants (NCCPA). To become certified, applicants must be graduates of an accredited PA program and pass the Physician Assistants National Certifying Examination. The examination consists of three parts: the first part tests general medical knowledge, the second section tests the PA's specialty—either primary care or surgery—and the third part tests for practical clinical knowledge. After successfully completing the examination, physician assistants can use the credential "Physician Assistant-Certified (PA-C)."

Once certified, PAs are required to complete 100 hours of continuing medical education courses every two years, and in addition must pass a recertification examination every six years. Besides NCCPA certification, most states also require that PAs register with the state medical board. State rules and regulations vary greatly concerning the work of PAs, and applicants are advised to study the laws of the state in which they wish to practice.

Exploring

Those interested in exploring the profession should talk with school guidance counselors, practicing PAs, PA students, and various health care employees at local hospitals and clinics. Students can also obtain information by contacting one of the organizations listed at the end of this chapter. Serving as a volunteer in a hospital, clinic, or nursing home is a good way for students to get exposure to the health care profession. In addition, while in college, students may be able to obtain summer jobs as hospital orderlies, nurse assistants, or medical clerks. Such jobs can help students assess their interest in and suitability for work as PAs before they apply to a PA program.

Employers

PAs work in a variety of health care settings. Most PAs, about 36 percent, are employed by single physicians, or group practices; three out of 10 are employed by hospitals. PAs also work in clinics and medical offices. They are employed by nursing homes, long-term care facilities, and prisons. Many areas lacking quality medical care personnel, such as remote rural areas and the inner city, are hiring PAs to meet their needs.

Starting Out

PAs must complete their formal training programs before entering the job market. Once their studies are completed, the placement services of the schools may help them find jobs. PAs may also seek employment at hospitals, clinics, medical offices, or other health care settings. Information about jobs with the federal government can be obtained by contacting the Office of Personnel Management.

Advancement

Since the PA profession is still quite new, formal lines of advancement have not yet been established. There are still several ways to advance. Hospitals, for example, do not employ head PAs. Those with experience can assume more responsibility at higher pay, or they move on to employment at larger hospitals and clinics. Some PAs go back to school for additional education to practice in a specialty area, such as surgery, urology, or ophthalmology.

Earnings

According to the American Academy of Physician Assistants, 80 percent of PA graduates find employment as a PA in less than a year. Salaries of PAs vary according to experience, specialty, and employer. In 1998, PAs earned a starting average of $62,294 annually. Those working in hospitals and medical offices earn slightly more than those working in clinics. Experienced PAs have the potential to earn close to $100,000 a year. PAs working for the military averaged $50,320 a year. PAs are well compensated compared with other occupations that have similar training requirements. Most PAs receive health and life insurance among other benefits.

Work Environment

Most work settings are comfortable and clean, although, like physicians, PAs spend a good part of their day standing or walking. The workweek varies according to the employment setting. A few emergency room PAs may work 24-hour shifts, twice a week; others work 12-hour shifts, three times a week. PAs who work in physicians' offices, hospitals, or clinics may have to work weekends, nights, and holidays. PAs employed in clinics, however, usually work five-day, 40-hour weeks.

Outlook

There were approximately 64,000 physician assistants employed in the United States in 1998. Employment for PAs, according to the U.S. Department of Labor, is expected to increase much faster than the average for all occupations. A 46.4 percent increase in the number of new jobs is projected through the year 2006. In fact, job growth is expected to outpace the number of potential employees entering this occupation by as much as 9 percent. This field was also mentioned in *U.S. News & World Report's* 1998 article, "Best Jobs for the Future."

The role of the PA in delivering health care has also expanded over the past decade. PAs have taken on new duties and responsibilities, and they now work in a variety of health care settings.

For More Information

The following organizations have information on physician assistant careers, education, and certification.

American Academy of Physician Assistants
950 North Washington Street
Alexandria, VA 22314
Tel: 703-836-2272
Email: aapa@aapa.org
Web: http://www.aapa.org

Association of Physician Assistant Programs
950 North Washington Street
Alexandria, VA 22314
Tel: 703-548-5538
Email: apap@aapa.org
Web: http://www.apap.org

National Commission on Certification of Physician Assistants
6849-B2 Peachtree Dunwoody Road
Atlanta, GA 30328
Tel: 404-493-9100
Web: http://www.social.com/health/nhicdata/hr1300/hr1334.html

Physicians

School Subjects	Biology Health
Personal Skills	Helping/teaching Technical/scientific
Work Environment	Primarily indoors Primarily multiple locations
Minimum Education Level	Medical degree
Salary Range	$44,400 to $160,000 to $250,000
Certification or Licensing	Required by all states
Outlook	Faster than the average

Overview

Physicians diagnose, prescribe medicines for, and otherwise treat diseases and disorders of the human body. A physician may also perform surgery and often specializes in one aspect of medical care and treatment. Physicians hold either a doctor of medicine (M.D.) or osteopathic medicine (D.O.) degree. (See *Osteopaths*)

History

The first great physician was Hippocrates, a Greek who lived almost 2,500 years ago. He developed theories about the practice of medicine and the anatomy of the human body, but Hippocrates is remembered today for a set of medical ethics that still influences medical practice. The oath that he administered to his disciples is administered to physicians about to start practice. His 87 treatises on medicine, known as the "Hippocratic Collection," are believed to be the first authoritative record of early medical theory and practice. Hippocratic physicians believed in the theory that health was maintained by a proper balance of four "humors" in the body: blood, phlegm, black bile, and yellow bile.

Another Greek physician, Galen (130?-201?) influenced medical thought for more than a thousand years. During the Middle Ages, his works were translated into Arabic and Syriac.

The great civilizations of Egypt, India, and China all developed medical theories of diagnosis and treatment that influenced later cultures of their own countries and those of other countries. The school of medicine at Alexandria, Egypt, for example, incorporated the theories of the ancient Greeks as well as those of the Egyptians. This great medical school flourished and was influential for several hundred years. Research specialists there learned more about human anatomy than had ever been learned before.

The theories and practices of medicine were kept alive almost entirely during the Middle Ages by monks in monasteries. Few new theories were developed during this period, but the medical records of most of the great early civilizations were carefully preserved and copied.

The Renaissance saw a renewal of interest in medical research. Swiss physician Parcelsus (1493-1541) publicly burned the writings of Galen and Avicena, signifying a break with the past. Concepts of psychology and psychiatry were introduced by Juan Luis Vives (1492-1540), a Spanish humanist and physician.

In the 17th century English physician William Harvey discovered that the blood, propelled by the pumping action of the heart, circulates through the body. Many inventions in other fields helped the progress of medicine. Anton van Leeuwenhoek (1632-1723), a Dutch lens grinder, made instruments that magnified up to 270 times. He also studied blood circulation and composition, and was the first to see bacteria and protozoans.

During the 18th century the Dutch physician Hermann Boerhaave introduced clinical instruction (teaching at the bedside of patients). Edward Jenner discovered a vaccination against smallpox. Specialization grew rapidly, as did the growth of medical schools, hospitals, and dispensaries.

The 19th century saw advances in more precise instruments, such as the stethoscope, the ophthalmoscope, and X rays. Doctors began to use anesthetics like ether and nitrous oxide and antiseptics. Knowledge of the cell, digestion, metabolism, and the vasomotor system increased.

Among the 20th century discoveries and developments have been the identification of four blood types, the discovery of insulin, development of antibiotics, and immunizations such as the polio vaccine. Technological advances have included the electron microscope, pacemakers, ultrasound, heart-lung machines, dialysis machines, and prostheses, to name only a few. Medical research and practice made giant strides toward the relief of human distress and the prolonging of human life. Every day brings new discoveries and the possibility of major breakthroughs in the areas that have long plagued humans.

The Job

The greatest number of physicians are in private practice. They see patients by appointment in their offices and examining rooms, and visit patients who are confined to the hospital. In the hospital, they may perform operations or give other kinds of medical treatment. Some physicians also make calls on patients at home if the patient is not able to get to the physician's office or if the illness is an emergency.

Approximately 15 percent of physicians in private practice are *general practitioners* or *family practitioners*. They see patients of all ages and both sexes and will diagnose and treat those ailments that are not severe enough or unusual enough to require the services of a specialist. When special problems arise, however, the general practitioner will refer the patient to a specialist.

Not all physicians are engaged in private practice. Some are in academic medicine and teach in medical schools or teaching hospitals. Some are engaged only in research. Some are salaried employees of health maintenance organizations or other prepaid health care plans. Some are salaried hospital employees.

Some physicians, often called *medical officers,* are employed by the federal government, in such positions as public health, or in the service of the Department of Veterans Affairs. State and local governments also employ physicians for public health agency work. A large number of physicians serve with the armed forces, both in this country and overseas.

Industrial physicians or *occupational physicians* are employed by large industrial firms for two main reasons: to prevent illnesses that may be caused by certain kinds of work and to treat accidents or illnesses of employees. Although most industrial physicians may roughly be classified as general practitioners because of the wide variety of illnesses that they must recognize and treat, their knowledge must also extend to public health techniques and to understanding such relatively new hazards as radiation and the toxic effects of various chemicals, including insecticides.

A specialized type of industrial or occupational physician is the *flight surgeon.* Flight surgeons study the effects of high-altitude flying on the physical condition of flight personnel. They place members of the flight staff in special low-pressure and refrigeration chambers that simulate high-altitude conditions and study the reactions on their blood pressure, pulse and respiration rate, and body temperature.

Another growing specialty is the field of nuclear medicine. Some large hospitals have a nuclear research laboratory, which functions under the direction of a chief of nuclear medicine, who coordinates the activities of the lab with other hospital departments and medical personnel. These physicians perform tests using nuclear isotopes and use techniques that let physicians see and understand organs deep within the body.

M.D.s may become specialists in any of the 40 different medical care specialties. Many of these specialties are discussed elsewhere in this book.

Requirements

High School

The physician is required to devote many years to study before being admitted to practice. Interested high school students should enroll in a college preparatory course, and take courses in English, languages (especially Latin), the humanities, social studies, and mathematics, in addition to courses in biology, chemistry, and physics.

Postsecondary Training

The student who hopes to enter medicine should be admitted first to a liberal arts program in an accredited undergraduate institution. Some colleges offer a "premedical" course, and it is advisable for the student to take such a course where it is offered. A good general education, however, with as many courses as possible in science and perhaps a major in biology, is considered adequate preparation for the study of medicine. Courses should include physics, biology, inorganic and organic chemistry, English, mathematics, and the social sciences.

College freshmen who hope to apply to a medical school early in their senior year should have adequate knowledge of the requirements for admission to one of the 125 accredited schools of medicine or 19 accredited schools of osteopathic medicine in the country. They should consult a copy of Medical School Admission Requirements, U.S. and Canada, available from the Association of American Medical Colleges. It is also available in college libraries. If students read carefully the admissions requirements of the several medical schools to which they hope to apply, they will avoid making mistakes in choosing a graduate program.

Students who do not enter a premedical program may find it possible to change to a major in biology or chemistry after they have enrolled. Such majors may make them eligible for consideration to be admitted to many medical schools.

Some students may be admitted to medical school after only three years of study in an undergraduate program. There are a few medical schools that will award the bachelor's degree at the end of the first year of medical school study. This practice is becoming less common as more students seek admission to medical schools. Most premedical students plan to spend four years in an undergraduate program and to receive the bachelor's degree before entering the four-year medical school program.

During the second or third year in college, undergraduates should arrange with an advisor to take the Medical College Admission Test (MCAT). This test is given each spring and each fall at certain selected sites. The student's advisor should know the date, place, and time; or the student may write for this information to the Association of American Medical Colleges. All medical colleges in this country require this test for admission, and a student's MCAT score is one of the factors that is weighed in the decision to accept or reject any applicant. Because the test does not evaluate medical knowledge, most college students who are enrolled in liberal arts programs should not find it to be unduly difficult. The examination covers four areas: verbal facility, quantitative ability, knowledge of the humanities and social sciences, and knowledge of biology, chemistry, and physics.

Students who hope to be admitted to medical school are encouraged to apply to at least three institutions to increase their chances of being accepted by one of them. Approximately one out of every two qualified applicants to medical schools will be admitted each year. To facilitate this process, the American Medical College Application Service (AMCAS) will check, copy, and submit applications to medical schools specified by the individual student. More information about this service may be obtained from AMCAS, premedical advisers, and medical schools.

In addition to the traditional medical schools, there are several schools of basic medical sciences that enroll medical students for the first two years (preclinical experience) of medical school. They offer a preclinical curriculum to students similar to that which is offered by a regular medical school. At the end of the two-year program, the student will then apply to a four-year medical school for the final two years of instruction.

Although high scholarship is a determining factor in admitting a student to a medical school, it is actually only one of the criteria considered. By far the greatest number of successful applicants to medical schools are "B" students. Because admission is also determined by a number of other factors, including a personal interview, other qualities in addition to a high scholastic average are considered desirable for a prospective physician. High on the list of desirable qualities are emotional stability, integrity, reliability, resourcefulness, and a sense of service.

The average student enters medical school at age 21 or 22. The student then begins another four years of formal schooling. During the first two years of medical school, the student learns human anatomy, biochemistry, physiology, pharmacology, psychology, microbiology, pathology, medical ethics, and laws governing medicine. Most instruction in the first two years is given through classroom lectures, laboratories, seminars, independent research, and the reading of textbook material and other types of literature. Students also learn to take medical histories, examine patients, and recognize symptoms.

During the last two years in medical school, the student becomes actively involved in the treatment process. Students spend a large proportion of the time in the hospital as part of a medical team headed by a teaching physician who specializes in a particular area. Others on the team may be interns or residents. Students are closely supervised as they learn techniques such as how to take a patient's medical history, how to make a physical examination, how to work in the laboratory, how to make a diagnosis, and how to keep all the necessary records.

Students rotate from one medical specialty to another, to obtain a broad understanding of each field. They are assigned to duty in internal medicine, pediatrics, psychiatry, obstetrics and gynecology, and surgery. Students may be assigned to other specialties, too.

In addition to this hospital work, students continue to take coursework. They are expected to be responsible for assigned studies and also for some independent study.

Most states require all new M.D.s to complete at least one year of postgraduate training, and a few require an internship plus a one-year residency. Physicians wishing to specialize spend from three to seven years in advanced residency training plus another two or more years of practice in the specialty. Then they must pass a specialty board examination to become a board-certified M.D. The residency years are stressful: residents often work 24-hour shifts and put in 80 hours or more per week.

For a teaching or research career, physicians may also earn a master's degree or a Ph.D. in biochemistry or microbiology.

Certification or Licensing

After receiving the M.D. degree, the new physician is required to take an examination to be licensed to practice. Every state requires such an examination. It is conducted through the board of medical examiners in each state.

Some states have reciprocity agreements with other states so that a physician licensed in one state may be automatically licensed in another without being required to pass another examination. Because this is not true throughout the United States, however, the wise physician will find out about licensing procedures before planning to move.

Other Requirements

Prospective physicians must have some plan for financing their long and costly education. They face a period of at least eight years after college when they will not be self-supporting. While still in school, students may be able to work only during summer vacations, because the necessary laboratory courses of the regular school year are so time consuming that little time is left for activities other than the preparation of daily lessons. Some scholarships and loans are available to qualified students.

Physicians who work directly with patients need to have great sensitivity to their needs. Interpersonal skills are required by all physicians, even in isolated research laboratories, since they must work and communicate with other scientists. Since new technology and discoveries happen at such a rapid rate, physicians must continually pursue further education to keep up with new treatments, tools, and medicines.

Exploring

One of the best introductions to a career in health care is to volunteer at a local hospital, clinic, or nursing home. In this way it is possible to get a feel for what it's like to work around other health care professionals and patients and possibly determine exactly where your interests lie. As in any career, reading as much as possible about the profession, talking with a high school counselor, and interviewing those working in the field are other important ways to explore your interest.

Employers

Physicians can find employment in a wide variety of settings, including hospitals, nursing homes, managed care offices, prisons, schools and universities, research laboratories, trauma centers, clinics, and public health centers.

Some are self-employed in their own or group practices. In the past, many physicians went into business for themselves, either by starting their own practice or by becoming a partner in an existing one. Very few physicians—about 6 percent—are choosing to follow this path today. There are a number of reasons for this shift. Often, the costs of starting a practice or buying into an existing practice are too high. Most are choosing to take salaried positions with hospitals or groups of physicians.

Jobs for physicians are available all over the world, although licensing requirements may vary. In Third World countries, there is great demand for medical professionals of all types. Conditions, supplies, and equipment may be poor and pay is minimal, but there are great rewards in terms of experience. Many doctors fulfill part or all of their residency requirements by practicing in other countries.

Physicians interested in teaching may find employment at medical schools or university hospitals. There are also positions available in government agencies such as the Centers for Disease Control, the National Institutes of Health, and the Food and Drug Administration.

Pharmaceutical companies and chemical companies hire physicians to research and develop new drugs, instruments, and procedures.

Starting Out

There are no shortcuts to entering the medical profession. Requirements are an M.D. degree, a licensing examination, a one- or two-year internship, and a period of residency that may extend as long as five years.

Upon completing this program, which may take up to 15 years, physicians are then ready to enter practice. They may choose to open a solo private practice, enter a partnership practice, enter a group practice, or take a salaried job with a managed care facility or hospital. Salaried positions are also available with federal and state agencies, the military, including the Department of Veterans Affairs, and private companies. Teaching and research jobs are usually obtained after other experience is acquired.

The highest ratio of physicians to patients is in the Northeast and West. The lowest ratio is in the South. Most M.D.s practice in urban areas near hospitals and universities.

Advancement

Physicians who work in a managed care setting or for a large group or corporation can advance by opening a private practice. Average physicians in a private practice do not advance in the accustomed sense of the word. Their progress consists of advancing in skill and understanding, in numbers of patients, and in income. They may be made a fellow in a professional specialty or elected to an important office in the American Medical Association or American Osteopathic Association. Teaching and research positions may also increase a physician's status.

Some physicians may become directors of a laboratory, managed care facility, hospital department, or medical school program. Some may move into hospital administration positions.

Physicians can achieve recognition by conducting research in new medicines, treatments, and cures, and publishing their findings in medical journals. Participation in professional organizations can also bring prestige.

A physician can advance by pursuing further education in a subspecialty or a second field such as biochemistry or microbiology.

Earnings

Physicians have among the highest average earnings of any occupational group. The level of income for any individual physician depends on a number of factors, such as region of the country, economic status of the patients, and the physician's specialty, skill, experience, professional reputation, and personality. Income tends to vary less across geographic regions, however, than across specialties. The median income after expenses for all physicians in 1995, according to the American Medical Association, was $160,000 per year. The median income of radiologists was $230,000; general surgeons, $225,000; family practitioners, $124,000; anesthesiologists, $203,000, and emergency medicine physicians, $170,000.

In 1996-97, the average first year resident received a stipend of about $32,789 a year, depending on the type of residency, the size of the hospital, and the geographic area. Sixth year residents earned about $40,849 a year. If the physician enters private practice, earnings during the first year may not be impressive. As the patients increase in number, however, earnings will also increase.

Physicians who complete their residencies but have no other experience begin work with the Department of Veterans Affairs at salaries of about $44,400 in addition to other cash benefits of up to $13,000.

Salaried doctors usually earn fringe benefits such as health and dental insurance, paid vacations, and the opportunity to participate in retirement plans.

Work Environment

The offices and examining rooms of most physicians are well equipped, attractive, well lighted, and well ventilated. There is usually at least one nurse-receptionist on the physician's staff, and there may be several nurses, a laboratory technician, one or more secretaries, a bookkeeper, or receptionist.

Physicians usually see patients by appointments that are scheduled according to individual requirements. They may reserve all mornings for hospital visits and surgery. They may see patients in the office only on certain days of the week.

Physicians spend much of their time at the hospital performing surgery, setting fractures, working in the emergency room, or visiting patients.

Physicians in private practice have the advantages of working independently, but most put in long hours—an average of 58 per week in 1994. Also, they may be called from their homes or offices in times of emergency. Telephone calls may come at any hour of the day or night. It is difficult for physicians to plan leisure-time activities, because their plans may change without notice. One of the advantages of group practice is that members of the group rotate emergency duty.

The areas in most need of physicians are rural hospitals and medical centers. Because the physician is normally working alone, and covering a broad territory, the workday can be quite long with little opportunity for vacation. Because placement in rural communities has become so difficult, some towns are providing scholarship money to students who pledge to work in the community for a number of years.

Physicians in academic medicine or in research have regular hours, work under good physical conditions, and often determine their own workload. Teaching and research physicians alike are usually provided with the best and most modern equipment.

Outlook

In the late 1990s, there were about 560,000 M.D.s and D.O.s working in the United States. Others are involved in research, teaching, administration, and consulting for insurance or pharmaceutical companies. About 70 percent of all physicians practice in offices. Others are on the staff of hospitals, or work in a variety of other health care facilities and in schools, prisons, and business firms.

This field is expected to grow faster than the average through the year 2006. Population growth, particularly among the elderly, is a factor in the demand for physicians. Another factor contributing to the predicted increase is the widespread availability of medical insurance, through both private plans and public programs. More physicians will also be needed for medical research, public health, rehabilitation, and industrial medicine. New technology will allow physicians to perform more procedures to treat ailments once thought incurable.

Employment opportunities will be good for family practitioners and internists, geriatric and preventive care specialists, as well as general pediatricians. Rural and low-income areas are in need of more physicians, and there is a short supply of general surgeons and psychiatrists.

The shift in health care delivery from hospitals to outpatient centers and other nontraditional settings to contain rising costs may mean that more and more physicians will become salaried employees. In 1994, for example, 39 percent of employed physicians were considered employees, rather than self-employed, up from 36 percent the previous year.

There will be considerable competition among newly trained physicians entering practice, particularly in large cities. Physicians willing to locate to inner cities and rural areas—where physicians are scarce—should encounter little difficulty.

The issue of physician oversupply has been addressed by groups such as the National Academy of Sciences Institute of Medicine and the Pew Health Professions Commission. They suggest limiting the number of future residency positions available to reduce the number of doctors vying for positions in the medical field.

For More Information

For career information, contact:

American Academy of Family Physicians
8880 Ward Parkway
Kansas City, MO 64114
Tel: 816-333-9700

American Medical Association
515 North State Street
Chicago, IL 60610
Tel: 312-464-5000
Web: http://www.ama-assn.org

For a list of accredited U.S. and Canadian medical schools and other education information, contact:

Association of American Medical Colleges
2450 N Street, NW
Washington, DC 20037
Tel: 202-828-0400
Web: http://www.aamc.org

Podiatrists

	School Subjects
Biology Health	
	Personal Skills
Helping/teaching Technical/scientific	
	Work Environment
Primarily indoors Primarily multiple locations	
	Minimum Education Level
Medical degree	
	Salary Range
$44,400 to $160,000 to $250,000	
	Certification or Licensing
Required by all states	
	Outlook
Faster than the average	

Overview

Podiatrists, or doctors of podiatric medicine, are specialists in diagnosing and treating disorders and diseases of the foot and lower leg. The most common problems that they treat are bunions, calluses, corns, warts, ingrown toenails, heel spurs, arch problems, and ankle and foot injuries. Podiatrists also treat deformities and infections. A podiatrist may prescribe treatment by medical, surgical, and mechanical or physical means.

The human foot is a complex structure, containing 26 bones plus muscles, nerves, ligaments, and blood vessels. The 52 total bones in your feet make up about one-fourth of all the bones in your body. Because of the foot's relation to the rest of the body, it may be the first body part to show signs of serious health conditions, such as diabetes or cardiovascular disease. Podiatrists may detect these problems first, making them an important part of the health care team.

History

Doctors who treat feet first began making rounds in larger U.S. cities in the early 1800s. During that century, podiatrists were called chiropodists, after the Greek word "chiropody." Chiropody refers to the study of the hand and foot. Most other physicians and surgeons of that era ignored the treatment of foot disorders.

The first offices devoted exclusively to foot care were established in 1841. The chiropodists of this period had difficulty competing with physicians in the care of ingrown toenails. The law read that a chiropodist had no right to make incisions involving the structures below the true skin. Treatments included removal of corns, warts, calluses, bunions, abnormal nails, and general foot care.

The term chiropody was eventually replaced by podiatry, likely because chiropody dealt mainly with the foot.

Modern podiatric medicine emerged in the early 1900s. More recently, surgery has become a necessary part of podiatric care. Today, the skills of podiatric physicians are in increasing demand, because foot disorders are among the most common and most often neglected health problems affecting people in the United States.

The Job

Podiatrists provide foot care in private offices, hospitals, ambulatory surgical centers, skilled nursing facilities, and treatment centers or clinics. They also work in the armed forces, government health programs, and on the faculty in health professional schools.

To diagnose a foot problem, the podiatrist may take X rays, perform blood tests, or prescribe other diagnostic tests. A main concern of the podiatrist is to keep people walking by eliminating pain and deformities. The ability to recognize other body disorders is a requirement for a podiatrist, as arthritis or diabetes may first appear in the feet. Circulation problems may also affect the feet first because they are farthest away from the heart's blood supply.

Treatment may involve fitting corrective devices, prescribing drugs and medications, ordering physical therapy, performing surgery, and prescribing corrective footgear.

Requirements

High School

High school students should take as many courses in biology, zoology, and inorganic and organic chemistry, and as much physics and math as possible to determine whether they have an interest in this field. The profession requires a scientific aptitude, manual dexterity, a good business sense, and an ability to put patients at ease.

Postsecondary Training

A minimum of 90 semester hours of prepodiatry education is required for entrance into a college of podiatric medicine. Over 90 percent of podiatric students have a bachelor's degree. Undergraduate work should include courses in English, chemistry, biology or zoology, physics, and mathematics.

There are seven accredited colleges offering the four-year course leading to a Doctor of Podiatric Medicine (D.P.M.). All colleges of podiatric medicine require the Medical College Admission Test (MCAT) as part of the application procedure. There is no schooling available in Canada, but an educational packet is available for students by writing to the Ontario Podiatric Medical Association.

The first two years in podiatry school are spent in classroom and laboratory work in anatomy, bacteriology, chemistry, pathology, physiology, pharmacology, and other basic sciences. In the final two years, students gain clinical experience in addition to their academic studies.

To practice in a specialty, podiatrists need an additional one to three years of postgraduate education, usually in the form of an office- or hospital-based residency.

Certification or Licensing

Podiatrists must be licensed in all 50 states, the District of Columbia, and Puerto Rico. A state board examination must be passed to qualify for licensing. Some states allow the exams to be taken during medical podiatric college, from the National Board of Podiatric Examiners, as a substitute for the state boards. About two-thirds of the states require applicants to serve an additional residency of at least one year.

Podiatrists may gain certification in one of three specialties: orthopedics, primary medicine, or surgery.

Other Requirements

The podiatrist must have a capacity to understand and apply scientific findings, the skill to manipulate delicate instruments, and, for those with their own practices, good business skills. Most importantly, they should like all kinds of people and have a sincere desire to help those needing care and attention.

Exploring

Students interested in podiatric medicine should arrange an interview with a trained podiatrist. To gain experience, they may obtain a summer job or volunteer their time in a clinic specializing in podiatric medicine.

Employers

A newly licensed podiatrist might begin working in a multispecialty group, a clinic, a hospital, or in an established solo or group podiatric medical practice. There are jobs for podiatrists in the armed forces, too. Most offices are found in large cities. The majority of podiatrists set up practices in the seven states where the colleges of podiatry are located (California, Florida, Illinois, Iowa, New York, Pennsylvania, and Ohio). Other states with a high number of podiatrists are New Jersey, Massachusetts, Michigan, and Texas.

Starting Out

College placement offices are usually the place to start the job search. Checking the classifieds in professional journals and applying directly to area clinics and practices are other ways to uncover job leads.

Advancement

Most podiatrists provide all types of foot care. However, some specialize in such areas as surgery (foot and ankle), orthopedics (bone, muscle, and joint disorders), podopediatrics (children's foot ailments), or podogeriatrics (foot disorders of the elderly).

Earnings

Podiatrists in well-established practices have incomes comparable to those earned by other well-paid professionals. For newly licensed podiatrists who have been in full-time practice for at least two years, the average income in 1997 was $61,000, according to the American Podiatric Medical Association. The association reported that median net income of podiatrists with 10 to 15 years of experience was $135,000.

Work Environment

Most podiatrists work independently in their own offices or in a group practice. The workweek is generally 40 to 44 hours per week. Podiatrists usually can set their own hours to coordinate office hours with hospital staff time or teaching schedules.

Outlook

In 1996, there were approximately 13,000 practicing podiatrists in the United States, according to the American Podiatric Medical Association.

Demand for podiatrists' skills is rapidly increasing, as the profession gains recognition as a health care specialty and as foot disorders become more widespread. More people are involved in sports and fitness programs, which can cause foot problems or make existing foot problems more apparent or unbearable. Also, a rapidly growing aging population, many of whom may have neglected their feet, will seek podiatric care. The demand for podiatric services is expected to grow even more as health insurance coverage for such care becomes widespread. Although foot care is not ordinarily covered by health insurance, Medicare and private insurance programs frequently cover acute medical and surgical foot services, as well as diagnostic X rays, fracture casts, and leg braces. Many HMOs and other prepaid plans provide routine foot care as well.

The outlook for podiatrists through the year 2006 is favorable throughout the country, but especially in the South and Southwest, where a shortage of practitioners exists.

Competition for residency positions is strong. If a state's licensing board requires residency, as two-thirds of the states currently do, it must be done before a podiatrist can begin practicing. With the heavy competition for these posts, it is unlikely that students with average grades will be able to secure employment in those states.

For More Information

For education and career information, contact the following organizations.

American Association of Colleges of Podiatric Medicine
1350 Piccard Drive, Suite 322
Rockville, MD 20850-4307
Tel: 301-990-6882
Web: http://www.aacpm.org

American Board of Podiatric Surgery
1601 Dolores Street
San Francisco, CA 94110-4906
Tel: 415-826-4640

American Podiatric Medical Association
9312 Old Georgetown Road
Bethesda, MD 20814-1621
Tel: 301-571-9200
Web: http://www.apma.org

Medical College Admission Test Program Office
PO Box 4056
2255 North Dubuque Road
Iowa City, IA 52243-4056
Tel: 319-337-1357

Canadian Podiatric Medical Association
45 Sheppard Avenue East, Suite 900
North York, ON M2N 5W9 Canada
Tel: 416-927-9111 or 888-220-3338

Psychiatrists

School Subjects
Health
Psychology
Sociology

Personal Skills
Helping/teaching
Technical/scientific

Work Environment
Primarily indoors
Primarily one location

Minimum Education Level
Medical degree

Salary Range
$137,200 to $150,900 to $207,500

Certification or Licensing
Required by all states

Outlook
Faster than the average

Overview

Psychiatrists are physicians who attend to patients' mental, emotional, and behavioral symptoms. They try to help people function better in their daily lives. Different kinds of psychiatrists use different treatment methods depending on their fields. They may explore a patient's beliefs and history. They may prescribe medicine, including tranquilizers, antipsychotics, and antidepressants. If they specialize in treating children, they may use play therapy.

History

The greatest advances in psychiatric treatment came in the latter part of the 19th century. Emil Kraepelin, a German psychiatrist, made an important contribution when he developed a classification system for mental illnesses that is still used for diagnosis. Sigmund Freud (1856-1939), the famous

Viennese psychiatrist, developed techniques for analyzing human behavior that have strongly influenced the practice of modern psychiatry. Freud first lectured in the United States in 1909. Swiss psychiatrist Carl Jung (1875-1961), a former associate of Freud's, revolutionized the field with his theory of a collective unconscious.

Another great change in treatment began in the 1950s with the development of medication that could be used in treating psychiatric problems, such as depression and anxiety.

The Job

Psychiatrists treat patients who suffer from mental and emotional illnesses that make it hard for them to cope with everyday living or to behave in socially acceptable ways. Problems treated range from being irritable and feeling frustrated to losing touch with reality. Some patients may abuse alcohol or drugs or commit crimes. Others may have physical symptoms that spring from mental or emotional disorders. Such disorders no longer are viewed with such shame as they were in the past. The more enlightened view of today is that emotional or mental problems need to be diagnosed and treated just like any other medical problem.

Some psychiatrists run general practices, treating patients with a variety of mental disorders. Others may specialize in certain types of therapy or kinds of patients; for example, the chronically ill.

Treatment varies according to patient needs. Psychiatrists may prescribe medication that affects the patient's mood or behavior, such as tranquilizers or antidepressants. Medication, an important part of treatment nowadays, may be used alone or with other treatment. Sometimes a psychiatrist may refer a patient to another psychiatrist well-versed in a particular treatment.

Psychiatrists must deal compassionately with patients who may be in bad shape physically as well as mentally. They may be homeless or suicidal, for example, and have neglected to take care of themselves. "I treat anything that a family practitioner would treat," says ward supervisor Dr. Jenny Kane. "If it's necessary, I call in a specialist."

Dr. Kane is one of a growing number of women joining the ranks of psychiatrists. The number of women psychiatrists has grown from 14.5 percent in 1982 to 25 percent in 1996, according to the American Psychiatric Association's 1996 National Survey of Psychiatric Practice.

The survey said that female psychiatrists see, on average, about 32 patients a week and male psychiatrists, about 37. Psychiatrists treat the largest number of their patients—36 percent—for mood disorders. The remainder of their caseloads is made up of patients with anxiety disorders (about 14 percent); schizophrenia, a condition where thoughts are disconnected and hallucinations may be seen and voices heard, and other psychoses, such as when a person is out of touch with reality (13 percent); infant, child, or adolescent disorders (10 percent); personality disorders (also 10 percent), other mental problems (7 percent); alcohol use problems (6 percent) and substance use disorders (4 percent), according to the survey.

Different kinds of psychiatrists use different methods to treat their patients. Behavior therapists use a carrot-and-stick method to change patients' behavior. They may also use meditation, relaxation, and other treatment methods, such as biofeedback, a process where patients use electronic monitors to measure the effects that their thoughts and feelings have on bodily functions like muscle tension, heart rate, or brain waves so that they can consciously control them through stress reduction.

Psychotherapists use what is often called "talking therapy." The therapist helps overcome emotional pain by helping the patient uncover and understand the feelings and ideas that form the root of the problem. Therapy is given to individuals, groups, couples, or families.

Psychoanalysts encourage the patient to talk freely or "free associate" in a form of psychotherapy to uncover troubling subconscious beliefs or conflicts and their causes. Dreams may also be examined for hints about the unconscious mind. Subconscious conflicts are believed to cause neurosis, which is an emotional disorder in which the patient commonly exhibits anxious behavior.

Child psychiatrists work with youth and usually their parents as well. At the opposite end of the age scale, other psychiatrists prefer to work with geriatric patients.

Industrial psychiatrists are employed by companies to deal with problems that affect employee performance, such as alcoholism or absenteeism.

Forensic psychiatrists work in the field of law. They evaluate defendants and testify on their mental state. They may help determine whether or not defendants understand the charges against them and if they can contribute to their own defense.

Psychologists also work with mentally or emotionally disturbed clients. They are not physicians, however, and cannot prescribe medication. In some cases, disturbed behavior results from disorders of the nervous system. These conditions are diagnosed and treated by neurologists, who are physicians specializing in problems of the nervous system.

Requirements

High School

High school students should enroll in college-preparatory programs, taking courses in English, languages, the humanities, social studies, mathematics, biology, chemistry, and physics.

Postsecondary Training

College freshmen should plan their undergraduate programs so they meet the admission requirements that are explained in the annual publication of the Association of American Medical Colleges, "Admission Requirements of American Medical Colleges Including Canada." During their second or third year in college, students should take the Medical College Admission Test, which most medical schools require.

In medical school, students must complete a four-year program of medical studies and supervised clinical work leading to their M.D. degrees.

New physicians who plan to specialize in psychiatry must complete a residency. In the first year, they work in several specialties, such as internal medicine and pediatrics. Then they work for three years in a psychiatric hospital or a general hospital's psychiatric ward. To become a child psychiatrist, for example, a doctor must train for at least three years in general residency and two years in child psychiatry residency. Psychiatrists who wish to become psychoanalysts spend six years in part-time training, either during or after residency. Part of their training involves undergoing psychoanalysis themselves.

After they complete their resident training in psychiatry, candidates take an intensive examination given by the Board of Psychiatry and Neurology, and if they pass, they become Diplomates in Psychiatry.

Certification or Licensing

Upon completion of the M.D., students must pass a test to be licensed to practice medicine in their states. Depending on the requirements of the state in which they plan to practice, they may be required to pass the National Board of Medical Examiners test, the Federal Licensing Examination, or an individual state licensing test.

Other Requirements

To complete the required studies and training, students need outstanding mental ability and perseverance. Psychiatrists must be emotionally stable so they can deal with their patients objectively. They must be able to listen well.

Exploring

Students who wish to find out more about the field of psychiatry should read all they can about it to get a feel for what the job entails. A recent book, *Career Planning for Psychiatrists* (1995), edited by Kathleen M. Mogul, M.D., and Leah J. Dickstein, M.D., provides a comprehensive guide to the various career opportunities available in psychiatry. Students also should talk with their high school counselors and take advantage of any chance to interview psychiatrists or other physicians.

It would also be helpful to volunteer or work part-time at hospitals, clinics, or nursing homes. College students may be able to find summer jobs as hospital orderlies, nurse's aides, or ward clerks.

Employers

According to the American Psychiatric Association's 1996 survey, about 40.5 percent of psychiatrists work mainly in solo office practice; 10 percent work in a group office practice. About 25 percent work at various kinds of hospitals, while about 12 percent work in a public clinic or outpatient facility. Smaller percentages work in private clinics and outpatient facilities, nursing homes, correctional facilities, health maintenance organizations, or other work settings. A majority of psychiatrists are connected in some way with a medical school, as volunteer or paid faculty members.

Starting Out

Psychiatrists in residency can find job leads in professional journals and through professional organizations such as the American Psychiatric Association. Many are offered permanent positions with the same institution where they complete their residency.

Advancement

Most psychiatrists advance in their careers by enlarging their knowledge and skills, clientele, and earnings. Those who work in hospitals, clinics, and mental health centers may become administrators. Those who teach or concentrate on research may become department heads.

Earnings

Psychiatrists' earnings are determined by the kind of practice they have and its location, their experience, and the number of patients they treat. Like other physicians, their average income is among the highest of any occupation.

Average income for psychiatrists is $137,200 a year, according to the American Medical Association. Psychiatrists in private practice earn about $148,800 a year, making higher average incomes than salaried employees working for hire, who earn an average of $127,500 a year.

Psychiatrists on staff at psychiatric facilities earn an average salary of $126,585, according to a 1997 salary survey by The National Association of Psychiatric Health Systems. Psychiatric medical directors at such facilities earn an average of $150,890 a year, according to the survey. Psychiatrists who serve soley as chief executive officers of psychiatric facilities and who are not medical directors earn an average of $197,834 a year. Those who are CEOs and also medical directors make the highest average salaries, $207,498 a year.

Work Environment

Psychiatrists in private practice set their own schedules and usually work regular hours. They may work some evenings or weekends to see patients who cannot take time off during business hours. Most psychiatrists, however, put in long workdays, averaging 52 hours a week, according to American Medical Association statistics. Like other physicians, psychiatrists are always on call. Dr. Kane likens the obligations of her job to parenting. "Whatever and whenever a patient needs me, it's my job to be there—or at least to make arrangements to have them taken care of," she says.

Psychiatrists in private practice typically work in comfortable office settings. Some private psychiatrists also work as hospital staff members, consultants, lecturers, or teachers.

Salaried psychiatrists work in private hospitals, state hospitals, and community mental health centers. They also work for government agencies, such as the U.S. Department of Health and Human Services, the Department of Defense, and the Veterans Administration.

Psychiatrists who work in public facilities often bear heavy workloads. Changes in treatment have reduced the number of patients in hospitals and have increased the number of patients in community health centers.

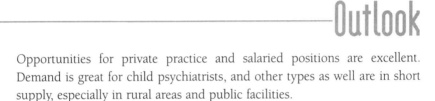

Outlook

Opportunities for private practice and salaried positions are excellent. Demand is great for child psychiatrists, and other types as well are in short supply, especially in rural areas and public facilities.

A number of factors contribute to this shortage. Growing population and increasing life span add up to more people who need psychiatric care; rising incomes enable more people to afford treatment; and higher educational levels make more people aware of the importance of mental health care. Medical insurance, although it usually limits the amount of mental health care, at least provides some coverage. However, the amount of benefits being paid out has been more than cut in half over the past 10 years.

Psychiatrists are also needed as researchers to explore the causes of mental illness and develop new ways to treat it.

For More Information

For information on choosing a medical specialty, as well as a description of psychiatry, please contact:

American Medical Association
515 North State Street
Chicago, IL 60610
Tel: 312-464-5000

Sports Physicians

Overview

Sports physicians treat patients who have sustained injuries to their musculoskeletal systems during the play or practice of an individual or team sporting event. Sports physicians also do preparticipation tests and physical exams. Some sports physicians create educational programs to help athletes prevent injury. Sports physicians work for schools, universities, hospitals, and private offices; some also travel and treat members of professional sports teams.

History

The field of sports medicine, and nearly all the careers related to it, owes its foundation to the experiments and studies conducted by Aristotle (384-322 BC), Leonardo da Vinci (1452-1519), and Etienne Jules Marey (1830-1904). Aristotle's treatise on the gaits of humans and animals established the beginning of biomechanics. In one experiment, he used the sun as a transducer to illustrate how a person, when walking in a straight line, actually throws a shadow that produces not a correspondingly straight line, but a zigzag line. Leonardo da Vinci's forays into the range and type of human motion explored a number of questions, including grade locomotion, wind resistance on the body, the projection of the center of gravity onto a base of support, and stepping and standing studies.

It was Marey, however, a French physiologist, who created much more advanced devices to study human motion. In fact, sports medicine and modern cinematography claim him as the father of their respective fields. Marey built the first force platform, a device which was able to visualize the forces between the foot and the floor. His nonphotographic studies of the gait of a horse inspired Eadward Muybridge's (1830-1904) serial photographs of a horse in motion, which in turn inspired Marey's invention of the chronophotograph. In contrast to Muybridge's consecutive frames, taken by several cameras, Marey's pictures with the chronophotograph superimposed the stages of action onto a single photograph; in essence, giving form to motion. By 1892, Marey had made primitive motion pictures, but his efforts were quickly eclipsed by those of Louis (1864-1948) and Auguste (1862-1954) Lumiere.

Following both World War I and II, Marey's and other scientists' experiments with motion would combine with medicine's need to heal and/or completely replace the limbs of war veterans. To provide an amputee with a prosthetic device that would come as close as possible to replicating the movement and functional value of a real limb, scientists and doctors began to work together at understanding the range of motion peculiar to the human body.

Mechanically, sports can be categorized according to the kinds of movements used. Each individual sport uses a unique combination of basic motions, including walking, running, jumping, kicking, and throwing. These basic motions have all been rigidly defined for scientific study so that injuries related to these motions can be better understood and treated. For example, sports that place heavy demands on one part of an athlete's body may overload that part and produce an injury, such as "tennis elbow" and "swimmer's shoulder." Baseball, on the other hand, is a throwing sport and certain injuries from overuse of the shoulder and elbow are expected. Athletes who play volleyball or golf also use some variation of the throwing motion and, therefore, also sustain injuries to their shoulders and elbows.

Today, sports medicine in particular deals with the treatment and prevention of injuries sustained while participating in sports and, as such, is not a single career but a group of careers that is concerned with the health of the athlete. For its specific purposes, the field of sports medicine defines "athlete" as both the amateur athlete who exercises for health and recreation, and the elite athlete who is involved in sports at the college, Olympic, or professional level. People of all ages and abilities are included, including those with disabilities.

Among the professions in the field of sports medicine are the trainer, physical therapist, physiologist, biomechanical engineer, nutritionist, psychologist, and physician. In addition, the field of sports medicine also encompasses the work of those who conduct research to determine the causes of sports injuries. Discoveries made by researchers in sports medicine have spread from orthopedics to almost every branch of medicine.

Arthroscopic surgery falls into this category. It was developed by orthopedic surgeons to see and operate on skeletal joints without a large open incision. The arthroscope itself is a slender cylinder with a series of lenses that transmit the image from the joint to the eye. The lens system is surrounded by glass fibers designed to transfer light from an external source to the joint. Inserted into the joint through one small, dime- to quarter-sized incision, the arthroscope functions as the surgeon's "eyes" to allow pinpoint accuracy when operating. The surgical elements, themselves, are inserted through other small incisions nearby. In the 1970s the techniques of arthroscopy were used by only a few surgeons as an exploratory measure to determine whether or not traditional, open surgery had a good chance of succeeding. Today, arthroscopy is the most common orthopedic surgery performed in the United States, and instead of being an exploratory procedure, 80 percent of all arthroscopic surgeries are performed to repair tissue damage.

The Job

Sports physicians treat the injuries and illnesses of both the amateur and elite athlete. They are often referred to as team physicians. Depending upon the level of athlete they are treating, sports physicians are usually either practitioners in family practice as medical doctors (M.D.s) or orthopedic surgeons. More often than not, the individual who works as the team physician for a professional sports team is too busy tending to the health needs of the team to have time for a private practice as well.

Brent Rich, M.D., Head Team Physician for Arizona State University and Team Physician for the Arizona Diamondbacks, agrees that there are some varieties of sports physicians: "Sports physicians come in two major varieties: primary care providers with training in non-surgical sports medicine and orthopedic surgeons. The majority of sports physicians are in private practice. Each area has its rewards and downfalls. As a board certified family physician, I deal with about 90 percent of what goes on in the sports medicine arena."

At the scholastic level, the team physician is usually the school physician and is appointed by the school board. Athletic programs at the collegiate level are usually capable of supporting a staff of one or more physicians who cater to the needs of the athletic teams. The size of the school and athletic program also determines the number of full-time physicians; for example, a state university basketball team might have one physician, even an orthopedic surgeon, dedicated wholly to that team's needs.

Professional teams, of course, have the necessary resources to employ both a full-time physician and an orthopedic surgeon. Generally, their presence is required at all practices and games. Often, professional teams have a sports medicine department to handle the various aspects of treatment, from training to nutrition to mental health. If they don't have their own department, they take advantage of the specialists at university hospitals and private care facilities in the area.

To fully understand the nature of a particular sports injury, sports physicians study the athlete as well as the sport. The musculoskeletal system is a complex organization of muscle segments, each related to the function of others through connecting bones and articulations. Pathological states of the musculoskeletal system are reflected in deficits (weaknesses in key muscle segments) that may actually be quite distant from the site of the injury or trauma. The risk factors for any given sport can be assessed by comparing the performance demands that regularly produce characteristic injuries with the risk factors that might predispose an athlete to injury.

Strength and flexibility, for example, are requirements for nearly every sport. Stronger muscles improve an athlete's performance, and deficits in strength can leave him or her prone to injury. Rehabilitation under the supervision of a sports physician focuses on rebuilding lost muscle strength. Likewise, an athlete who lacks flexibility may subject him or herself to strains or pulls on her muscles. For this athlete, rehabilitation would center on warming and stretching the isolated muscles, as well as muscle groups, to reduce or alleviate such muscle strains. In both cases, it is the responsibility of the sports physician to analyze the potential for injury and work with other sports health professionals to prevent it, as well as to treat the injury after it happens. The goal of every sports physician is to keep athletes performing to the best of their ability and to rehabilitate them safely and quickly after they are injured.

To prevent injuries, as well as treat them, sports physicians administer or supervise physical examinations of the athletes under their care to determine the fitness level of each athlete prior to that athlete actively pursuing the sport. During the exams, sports physicians note any physical traits, defects, previous injuries, or weaknesses. They also check the player's maturity, coordination, stamina, balance, strength, and emotional state. The physical examination accomplishes many different goals. To begin with, it quickly establishes the athlete's state of health and allows the sports physician to determine whether that athlete is physically capable of playing his or her sport. On the basis of the physical exam, the sports physician advises the coach on the fitness level of the athlete which, of course, determines a great deal about the athlete's position on the team. Furthermore, the exam alerts the sports physician to signs of injury, both old and new. Old or existing injuries can be noted and put under observation, and weaknesses can be detected early on so that proper conditioning and training patterns can be implemented by the coach and trainers.

Depending upon the results of their physical examinations, the sports physician may advise athletes to gain or lose weight, change their eating, drinking, and sleeping habits, or alter their training programs to include more strength or cardiovascular exercises. Routine physical checkups are also a common way of evaluating an athlete's performance level throughout a season, and many sports physicians will administer several exams to gauge the effect of their advice, as well as to ensure that the athlete is making the suggested changes in habits or training.

Preventing injuries is the sports physician's first goal and conditioning is probably the best way to accomplish that goal. Sports physicians are often responsible for developing and supervising the conditioning and training programs that other sports health professionals will implement. The sports physician may work with the coaching staff and athletic trainers to help athletes develop strength, cardiovascular fitness, and flexibility, or the sports physician may advise the coaching and training staff members of the overall safety of a practice program. For example, the sports physician may evaluate the drills and practice exercises that a football coach is using on a given day to make certain that the exercises won't exacerbate old injuries or cause new ones. Sports physicians may even be involved in the selection of protective gear and equipment. The degree of their involvement, again, depends on the size of the team and the nature of the physicians' skills or expertise, as well as on the number of other people on the staff. Large, professional teams tend to have equally large staffs on which one person alone is responsible for ordering and maintaining the protective gear, for example.

Sports physicians are often in attendance at practices (or they are nearby, in case of an injury), but their presence at games is mandatory. If a player shows signs of undue fatigue, exhaustion, or injury, the sports physician needs to be there to remove the athlete from the competition. Dr. Rich says being at the games is one of the perks of his profession: "To see others accomplish what they desire gives me satisfaction. Another good part is covering sports events and feeling a part of the action on the sidelines, in the locker room, or in the heat of the battle."

After an athlete is injured, the sports physician must be capable of immediately administering first-aid or other procedures. He or she first examines the athlete to determine the gravity and extent of the injury. If the damage is extreme enough (or cannot be determined from a manual and visual exam), the sports physician may send the athlete to the hospital for X rays or other diagnostic examinations. Later, the team physician may perform surgery, or recommend that the athlete undergo treatment or surgery by a specialist. Some of the most common types of injuries are stress fractures, knee injuries, back injuries, shoulder injuries, and elbow injuries.

The sports physician oversees the athlete's recuperation and rehabilitation following an injury, including the nature and timing of physical therapy. The athlete's return to practice and competition is determined by the sports physician's analysis of the athlete's progress. Frequent physical examinations allow the physician to judge whether or not the athlete is fit enough to return to full activity. The decision to allow an athlete to compete again following an injury is a responsibility that sports physicians take seriously; whether the athlete is an amateur or an elite professional, the future health and well-being of the athlete is at stake and cannot be risked, even for an important championship game.

A developing area of the sports physician's responsibilities is the diagnosis and treatment of substance abuse problems. Unfortunately, even as research on the field of sports medicine has produced new methods and medications that mask pain and decrease inflammation—which shortens recovery time and lengthens athletic careers—some also produce unnatural performance enhancement. Most notable of these are anabolic steroids—synthetic modifications of the male hormone, testosterone—which have become widely abused by athletes who use them to better their performances. When taken while on a high protein diet and an intensive exercise regimen, these drugs can increase muscle bulk, which in turn can produce increased strength, speed, and stamina. The side effects of these drugs, however, include aggression, sterility, liver problems, premature closure of the growth plates of the long bones, and in women, male pattern baldness and facial hair. These side effects are usually irreversible and, as such, pose a significant health risk for young athletes.

Another method also banned from use in competition-level athletics is the withdrawal of an athlete's blood several weeks prior to competition. The blood is stored and then, just before the athlete competes, the blood is transfused back into his or her bloodstream. This process, blood doping, also has serious, even fatal, side effects, including heart failure and death.

Finally, professional athletes sometimes develop substance abuse problems, such as alcohol or drug use. Sports physicians are responsible for detecting all of these problems and helping the athlete return to a healthy lifestyle, which may include competition.

In addition to the responsibilities and duties outlined above, many sports physicians also perform clinical studies and work with researchers to determine ways of improving sports medicine practices. Often, the results of such studies and research are published in medical journals and even popular magazines.

Requirements

High School

During high school, take as many health and sports-related classes as possible. Biology, chemistry, health, computers, and English are important core courses. High grades in high school are important for anyone aspiring to join the medical profession, because competition for acceptance into medical programs at colleges and universities is always tough.

Postsecondary Training

Sports physicians have either an M.D. (medical doctor degree) or a D.O. (doctor of osteopathy degree). Each involves completing four years of college, followed by four years of medical school, study, and internship at an accredited medical school, and up to six years of residency training in a medical specialty, such as surgery. Many physicians also complete a fellowship in sports medicine either during or after their residency.

During the first two years of medical school, medical students usually spend most of their time in classrooms learning anatomy, physiology, biology, and chemistry, among other subjects. In their last two years, they begin seeing patients in a clinic, observing and working with doctors to treat patients and develop their diagnostic skills. Some medical schools are beginning to alter this time-honored tradition by having the medical students begin to work with patients much sooner than two years into their schooling, but this method of combining classroom and clinical experiences is not yet fully accepted or integrated into the curriculum.

After medical school, the new doctors spend a year in an internship program, followed by several years in a residency training program in their area of specialty. Most sports physicians complete this stage of their training by working in orthopedics or general practice.

The fellowship portion of a doctor's training is essential if he or she has chosen to specialize. For example, the doctor specializing in general surgery and interested in sports medicine would probably seek an orthopedics fellowship providing further training in orthopedic surgery techniques.

Certification or Licensing

Finally, to become licensed, doctors must have completed the above training in accordance with the guidelines and rules of their chosen area or specialty. Beyond the formal requirements, this usually involves a qualifying written exam, followed by in-depth oral examinations designed to test the candidate's knowledge and expertise.

Other Requirements

Sports physicians must be able to learn and remember all the many parts and variations about the human body and how it functions. Knowledge of different sports and their demands on an athlete's body is also important. Like all medical doctors, sports physicians need to be able to communicate clearly to their patients with compassion and understanding.

Exploring

High school students interested in becoming sports physicians should look into the possibility of working with the physician, coach, or athletic trainer for one of their school's teams. Firsthand experience is the best way to gain fresh perspective into the role of the team physician. Later on, when applying for other paid or volunteer positions, it will help to have already had sports-related experience. Dr. Rich agrees, "Try to get experience with a physician who does what you think you want to do. Spending time in their offices, in surgery, or on the sidelines at high school games will give you exposure. As you learn more, you can do more."

Employers

Most sports physicians are in private practice, so they work for themselves or with other medical doctors. Some sports physicians, however, may work for sports clinics, rehabilitation centers, hospitals, and college/university teaching hospitals. Still other sports physicians travel with professional baseball, basketball, football, hockey, and soccer teams to attend to those specific athletes. Sports physicians are employed all over the country.

Starting Out

You won't become the team physician for a National Basketball Association team fresh out of medical school. Many sports physicians begin by joining an existing practice and volunteering with a local sports organization. After several years they may apply to the school board for consideration as a team physician for their local school district. Later, they may apply for a position with a college team until they ultimately seek a position with a national or international professional athletics team or organization. This gradual climb occurs while the individual also pursues a successful private practice and builds a strong, solid reputation. Often, the sports physician's established reputation in an area of specialty draws the attention of coaches and management looking to hire a physician for their team. Others take a more aggressive and ambitious route and immediately begin applying for positions with various professional sports teams as an assistant team physician. As in any other field, contacts can prove to be extremely useful, as are previous experiences in the field. For example, a summer volunteership or internship during high school or college with a professional hockey team might lead to a job possibility with that hockey team years later. Employment opportunities depend on the skill and ambitions of each job candidate.

Advancement

Depending on the nature of an aspiring sports physician's affiliation with athletic organizations (part time or full time), advancement paths will vary. For most sports physicians, advancement will accompany the successful development of their private practices. For those few sports physicians who are employed full time by professional athletic organizations, advancement from assistant to team physician is usually accompanied by increased responsibilities and a corresponding increase in salary.

Earnings

The earnings of a sports physician vary depending upon his or her responsibilities and the size and nature of the team. The private sports physician of a professional individual athlete, such as a figure skater or long distance runner, will most likely earn far less than the team physician for a professional football or basketball team, primarily because the earnings of the team are so much greater that the organization can afford to pay more for the physician's services. On the other hand, the team physician for the professional basketball team probably wouldn't have time for a private practice, although the sports physician for the figure skater or runner would, in all likelihood, also have a private practice or work for a sports health facility.

According to the American Medical Association, general practitioners and family practice physicians earn an annual net income of approximately $112,000, not including the fees and other income paid to them by the various athletic organizations for whom they work as team physicians. Again, these fees will vary according to the size of the team, the location, and the level of the athletic organization (high school, college, or professional being the most common). The income generated from these fees is far less than what they earn in their private practices. On the other hand, those team physicians who are employed full time by a professional organization will likely make more than their nonprofessional sports counterparts, even as much as one million dollars or more.

Work Environment

Sports physicians must be ready for a variety of work conditions, from the sterile, well-lighted hospital operating room to the concrete bleachers at an outdoor municipal swimming pool. The work environment is as diverse as the sports in which athletes are involved. Although most of their day-to-day responsibilities will be carried out in clean, comfortable surroundings, on game day they are expected to be where the athletes are, and that might be a muddy field (football and soccer); a snow-covered forest (cross-country skiing); a hot, dusty track (track and field); or a steamy ring (boxing). Picture the playing field of any given sport and that is where you will find sports physicians. They are also expected to travel with the athletes whenever they go out of town. This means being away from their home and family, often for several days, depending on the nature, level, and location of the competition.

Outlook

After years of watching athletes like Babe Ruth close down the bars after a game, coaches and management now realize the benefits of good health and nutrition. Within the world of professional sports, the word is out: proper nutrition, conditioning, and training prevent injuries to athletes, and preventing injuries is the key when those athletes are making their owners revenues in the billions of dollars. A top sports physician, then, is a worthwhile investment for any professional team. Thus, the outlook for sports physicians remains strong.

Even outside the realm of professional sports, amateur athletes require the skills and expertise of talented sports physicians to handle the aches and pains that come from pulling muscles and overtaxing aging knees. Athletes of all ages and abilities take their competitions seriously, and are as prone to injury as any pro athlete, if not more, because amateur athletes in general spend less time conditioning their bodies.

For More Information

To obtain publications about sports medicine, contact:

American College of Sports Medicine
PO Box 1440
Indianapolis, IN 46206-1440
Tel: 317-637-9200, ext. 117
Email: pip2acsm@acsm.org
Web: http://www.a1.com/sportsmed/index.html

For a list of accredited athletic training programs, job listings, and information on certification, contact:

National Athletic Trainers Association (NATA)
2952 Stemmons Freeway
Dallas, TX 75247-6196
Tel: 214-637-6282
Web: http://www.nata.org

American Orthopaedic Society for Sports Medicine
6300 North River Road, Suite 200
Rosemont, IL 60018
Tel: 847-292-4900
Email: aossm@aossm.org
Web: http://www.sportsmed.org

American Physical Therapy Association
1111 North Fairfax Street
Alexandria, VA 22314
Tel: 703-684-APTA (2782)
Web: http://www.apta.org

To join a forum on various medical issues, visit the AMA's Web site:

American Medical Association
515 North State Street
Chicago, IL 60610
Tel: 312-464-5000
Web: http://www.ama-assn.org

Surgeons

School Subjects
Biology
Health

Personal Skills
Helping/teaching
Technical/scientific

Work Environment
Primarily indoors
Primarily multiple locations

Minimum Education Level
Medical degree

Salary Range
$44,400 to $160,000 to $250,000

Certification or Licensing
Required by all states

Outlook
Faster than the average

Overview

Surgeons are physicians who make diagnoses and provide preoperative, operative, and postoperative care in surgery affecting almost any part of the body. These doctors also work with trauma victims and the critically ill.

History

Surgery is perhaps the oldest of all medical specialties. Evidence from Egypt, Greece, China, and India suggests that humans have always performed and worked on developing surgical procedures.

The field of surgery advanced during the 18th century when knowledge of anatomy increased through developments in pathology. At this time, common procedures included amputations as well as tumor and bladder stone removal. Surgery patients were usually tied down or sedated with alcoholic beverages or opium during the procedures.

The late 19th century brought major developments that advanced surgical procedures. Anesthesia was introduced in 1846. Also, Louis Pasteur's understanding of bacteria later resulted in the development of antiseptic by Joseph Lister in 1867. The introduction of anesthesia coupled with the use of antiseptic methods resulted in the new phase of modern surgery.

Surgical advances during the 20th century include the separation of surgical specialties, the development of surgical tools and X rays, as well as continued technological advances that create alternatives to traditional procedures, such as laparoscopic surgery with lasers.

The Job

The work of a surgeon will vary according to the work environment. For example, a general surgeon who specializes in trauma care would most likely work in a large, urban hospital where he or she would spend a great deal of time in the operating room performing emergency surgical procedures at a moment's notice. On the other hand, a general surgeon who specializes in hernia repair would probably have a more predictable work schedule and would spend most of the time in an ambulatory (also called outpatient) surgery center.

The surgeon is responsible for the diagnosis of the patient, for performing operations, and for providing patients with postoperative surgical care and treatment. In emergency room situations, the patient typically comes in complaining of some type of severe pain. If the patient needs surgery, the on-duty general surgeon will schedule the surgery. Depending on the urgency of the case, surgery may be scheduled for the following day or the patient will be operated on immediately.

A surgeon sees such cases as gunshot, stabbing, and accident victims. Other cases that often involve emergency surgery include appendectomies, removal of the spleen, and removal of kidney stones. When certain problems, such as a kidney stone or inflamed appendix, are diagnosed at an early stage, the surgeon can perform nonemergency surgery.

There are several specialties of surgery and four areas of subspecialization of general surgery. For these areas, the surgeon can receive further education and training leading to certification. A few of these specializations are *neurosurgery* (care for disorders of the nervous system), *plastic and reconstructive surgery* (care for defects of the skin and underlying musculoskeleton), *orthopaedic surgery* (care for musculoskeletal disorders that are present at birth or develop later), and *thoracic surgery* (care for diseases and conditions of the chest). The subspecializations for general surgery are: general vascular surgery, pediatric surgery, hand surgery, and surgical critical care.

Requirements

Postsecondary Training

To become a surgeon you must first earn an M.D. degree and become licensed to practice medicine (See *Physicians*). Physicians wishing to pursue general surgery must complete a five-year residency in surgery according to the requirements set down by the Accreditation Council for Graduate Medical Education (ACGME) and the Royal College of Physicians and Surgeons of Canada.

Throughout the surgery residency, residents are supervised at all levels of training by assisting on and then performing basic operations, such as the removal of an appendix. As the residency years continue, residents gain responsibility through teaching and supervisory duties. Eventually the residents are allowed to perform complex operations independently.

Subspecialties require from one to three years of additional training.

Certification and Licensing

Board certification in surgery is administered by the American Board of Surgery, Inc. While certification is a voluntary procedure, it is highly recommended. Most hospitals will not grant privileges to a surgeon without board certification. HMOs and other insurance groups will not make referrals or payments to a surgeon without board certification. Also, insurance companies are not likely to insure a surgeon for malpractice if he or she is not board certified.

To be eligible to apply for certification in surgery, a candidate must have successfully completed medical school and the requisite residency in surgery. Once a candidate's application has been approved, the candidate may take the written examination. After passing the written exam, the candidate may then take the oral exam.

Certification in surgery is valid for 10 years. To obtain recertification, surgeons must apply to the American Board of Surgery, Inc. with documentation of their continuing medical education activities and of the operations and procedures they have performed since being certified, and submit to a review by their peers. They must also pass a written exam.

Other Requirements

To be a successful surgeon, you should be able to think quickly and act decisively in stressful situations, enjoy helping and working with people, have strong organizational skills, be able to give clear instructions, have good hand-eye coordination, and be able to listen and communicate well.

Earnings

According to a 1998 survey conducted by the American Medical Association, the average net pay for surgeons is about $275,200, but salaries may begin at roughly $137,700. Incomes may vary from specialty to specialty. Other factors influencing individual incomes include the type and size of practice, the hours worked per week, the geographic location, and the reputation a surgeon has among both patients and fellow professionals.

Outlook

The wide-ranging skills and knowledge of the surgeon will always be in demand, whether or not the surgeon has a subspecialty. According to the *Occupational Outlook Handbook,* physician jobs are expected to grow faster than the average through the year 2006. The job outlook for surgeons is expected to match this trend, and positions are projected to grow at a faster than average rate.

For More Information

Following are organizations that provide information on the position of surgeon. In particular, the Association of Women Surgeons publishes a guide for women in the surgical specialties, A Manual for Surgical Interns and Residents.

American Board of Surgery, Inc.
1617 John F. Kennedy Boulevard, Suite 860
Philadelphia, PA 19103
Tel: 215-568-4000
Web: http://www.absurgery.org

Association of Women Surgeons
414 Plaza Drive, Suite 209
Westmont, IL 60559
Tel: 630-655-0392

Society of Thoracic Surgeons
401 North Michigan Avenue
Chicago, IL 60611
Tel: 312-644-6610
Web: http://www.sba.com

American Academy of Orthopaedic Surgeons
6300 North River Road
Rosemont, IL 60018-4262
Tel: 847-823-7186
Web: http://www.aaos.org

American Board of Plastic Surgery
1635 Market Street, Suite 400
Philadelphia, PA 19103-2204
Tel: 215-587-9322
Web: http://www.abplsurg.org

American Association of Neurological Surgeons
22 South Washington Street
Park Ridge, IL 60068
Tel: 847-692-9500
Web: http://www.neurosurgery.org

Urologists

School Subjects
| Biology
| Health

Personal Skills
| Helping/teaching
| Technical/scientific

Work Environment
| Primarily indoors
| Primarily multiple locations

Minimum Education Level
| Medical degree

Salary Range
| $44,400 to $160,000 to $250,000

Certification or Licensing
| Required by all states

Outlook
| Faster than the average

Overview

Urologists are physicians who specialize in the treatment of medical and surgical disorders of the adrenal gland and of the genitourinary system. They deal with the diseases of both the male and female urinary tract and of the male reproductive organs.

History

Medieval "healers" who specialized in the surgical removal of bladder stones could be considered the first "urologists," but due to his 1958 documentation of urethra, bladder, and kidney diseases, Francisco Diaz is the recognized founder of modern urology.

Advancements in urology came during the 19th century when flexible catheters were invented to examine and empty the bladder. In 1877, Max Nitze developed the lighted cytoscope, which is used to view the interior of the bladder. By the 20th century, diseases of the urinary tract could be diagnosed by X ray.

The Job

Technically, urology is a surgical subspecialty, but because of the broad range of clinical problems they treat, urologists also have a working knowledge of internal medicine, pediatrics, gynecology, and other specialties.

Common medical disorders that urologists routinely treat include prostate cancer, testicular cancer, bladder cancer, stone disease, urinary tract infections, urinary incontinence, and impotence. Less common disorders include kidney cancer, renal (kidney) disease, male infertility, genitourinary trauma, and sexually transmitted diseases (including AIDS).

The management and treatment of malignant diseases constitute much of the urologist's practice. Prostate cancer is the most common cancer in men, and the second leading cause of cancer deaths in men. If detected early, prostate cancer is treatable, but once it has spread beyond the prostate it is difficult to treat successfully.

Testicular cancer is the leading cause of cancer in young men between the ages of 15 and 34. Major advances in the treatment of this cancer, involving both surgery and chemotherapy, now make it the most curable of all cancers. Bladder cancer occurs most frequently in men age 70 and older, and treatment for it also has a high success rate.

Young and middle-aged adults are primarily affected by stone diseases, which represent the third leading cause of hospitalizations in the United States. Kidney stones, composed of a combination of calcium and either oxalate or phosphate, usually pass through the body with urine. Larger stones, however, can block the flow of urine or irritate the lining of the urinary system as they pass. What has become standard treatment today is called extracorporeal shock wave lithotripsy (ESWL). In ESWL, high-energy shock waves are used to pulverize the stones into small fragments that are carried from the body in the urine. This procedure has replaced invasive, open surgery as the preferred treatment for stone disease.

Urologists also consult on spina bifida cases in children and multiple sclerosis cases in adults, as these diseases involve neuromuscular dysfunctions that affect the kidneys, bladder, and genitourinary systems.

The scope of urology has broadened so much that the following are now considered subspecialties: pediatric urology, urologic oncology, and female urology.

Requirements

Postsecondary Training

To become a urologist you must first earn an M.D. degree and become licensed to practice medicine. (See *Physicians*) Then you must complete a five- or six-year residency in urology, of which the first two years are typically spent in general surgery, followed by three to four years of urology in an approved residency program. Currently, there are 116 approved residency programs.

Many urologic residency training programs are six years in length, with the final year spent in either research or additional clinical training, depending on the orientation of the program and the resident's focus.

The vast majority of urologists enter into clinical practice after completing their residency program. However, fellowships exist in various subspecialties, including pediatrics, infertility, sexual dysfunction, oncology, and transplantation.

Certification or Licensing

At an early point in the residency period, all students are required to pass a medical licensing examination administered by the board of medical examiners in each state. The length of the residency depends on the specialty chosen.

Certification requires the successful completion of a qualifying written examination, which must be taken within three years of completing the residency in urology. The subsequent certifying examination, which consists of pathology, uroradiology, and a standardized oral examination, must be taken within five years of the qualifying examination. Certification by the American Board of Urology is for a 10-year period, with recertification required after that time.

Other Requirements

Urologists should like working with people and have a strong interest in promoting good health through preventive measures such as diet and exercise.

The urologist diagnoses and treats conditions of a very personal nature. Many patients are uncomfortable talking about problems relating to their kidneys, bladder, or genitourinary system. The urologist must show compassion and sensitivity to dispel the patient's fears and put him or her at ease.

Excellent communication skills are essential to patient-physician interactions. Urologists should be able to clearly articulate both the patient's problem and the recommended forms of treatment, including all of the options and their attendant risks and advantages. Because of their frequent consultations with other physicians, urologists also need to develop good working relationships with other medical specialists.

Urologists, like all surgeons, should be in good physical condition; they must remain steady and focused while standing for hours on their feet. Urologists who work in hospital trauma units should be prepared for the frenetic pace and tension of split-second decision making.

Earnings

According to a 1998 survey conducted by the American Medical Association, the average net salary of practitioners of internal medicine is about $185,700, but salaries may begin around $116,306. These figures pertain to doctors of internal medicine, and income for urologists may vary from these numbers. The average net pay for surgeons is about $275,200.

Outlook

Employment prospects for urologists are good. According to the *Occupational Outlook Handbook,* physicians' jobs are expected to grow faster than the average through 2006. The demographics of American society illustrate that the increase in the aging population will increase demand for services that cater, in large part, to them. With baby boomers aging, the need for qualified urologists will continue to grow.

For More Information

For additional information on becoming a urologist, contact the following:

American Medical Association
515 North State Street
Chicago, IL 60610
Tel: 312-464-5000
Web: http://www.ama-assn.org

American Board of Urology
2216 Ivy Road, Suite 210
Charlottesville, VA 22903
Tel: 248-646-9720

American Urological Association, Inc.
1120 North Charles Street
Baltimore, MD 21201
Tel: 410-727-1100
Web: http://www.auanet.org

Index